"for persons beginning to discover
the Episcopal Church"

W9-ATM-307

Looking
at the
Episcopal
Church

William Sydnor

MOREHOUSE PUBLISHING

The stanzas reproduced from the hymn "God My Father, Loving Me" by G. W. Briggs are taken from *Enlarged Songs of Praise* and used with permission of Oxford University Press.

Ninth printing, 1996

Morehouse Publishing
Editorial Office
871 Ethan Allen Highway
Ridgefield, CT 06877

Corporate Office
P.O. Box 1321
Harrisburg, PA 17105

ISBN 0-8192-1279-2
Library of Congress Catalog Card Number 80-81103

Printed in the United States of America

To my cosmopolitan grandchildren
who amaze and awe and humble me

Caroline
Berkely
Tom
Bryan
Jyoti

Other Books by William Sydnor

How & What the Church Teaches
Introductions to the Scripture Read in Worship
Jesus According to Luke
Keeping the Christian Year
More Than Words
The Son of God (with Edric Weld)
The Story of the Real Prayer Book
Sunday's Scriptures
Traveling the Way (with Drusilla McGowen)
Your Voice, God's Word

Contents

Preface

There is a need for a simple, not-too-detailed account of the facts about the Episcopal Church. That is what, God willing, this book is intended to be. In another day there were books such as Lefferd M. A. Haughwout, *The Ways and Teachings of the Church* which filled that need for a number of people. Perhaps this effort to lead inquirers from superficial appearance to meaning to commitment will in some way fill that need in this present time. At the least, it is an effort to provide material to put into the hands of persons who are beginning to discover the Episcopal Church.

Among those inquirers are that restless tribe of noisy future church leaders known as "Confirmation Age Children." Because it is possible that the material here may, in the wisdom of the rector, form the basis of a course of Confirmation instruction for such youngsters, a leader's guide has been included as an appendix to assist the person responsible for conducting that class. I hope it conveys something of the sense of privilege and excitement that goes with sharing this time with growing young church people.

I am indebted to many people for the insights and information presented here. Those with special expertise of one kind or another include the Rev. Charles P. Price, Professor of Theology, Virginia Theological Seminary, Miss Kristen Leigh Mulvaney whose knowledge of adolescents far surpasses mine, the Rt. Rev. Robert F. Gibson, Jr., retired Bishop of Virginia, who has for years hidden his authoritative knowledge of Church history under a miter, Mrs. Harold C. Kelleran, and the Rev. William L. Dols, rector of Immanuel-on-the-Hill, Alexandria, Virginia, who are walking compendia of creative Christian education procedures. These friends have been generous with their knowledge and gentle with their advice. And I am blessed with a wife who understands firsthand about the demands of writing a book.

William Sydnor

Alexandria, Va.
August 5, 1980

PART ONE

*When we look at the
Episcopal Church we are
first impressed with
those things that meet
the eye—the building,
outside and in . . . the
decorations . . . symbols
. . . vestments . . .ser-
vices, regular and those
occasionally observed . . .
the behavior of the
people. Let's consider
something of the meaning
of these. . . .*

. . . FIRST APPEARANCES.

Chapter 1

How the Church Looks to Outsiders

That church on the corner is no ordinary building. It is a "special place" to those who worship there on Sunday and participate in other activities there during the week. Inside, its furniture, its walls, its windows are decorated with symbols and pictures, carvings and needlework, all of which have meaning for those who belong. The people who worship there take part in services from which they gain inspiration and guidance, a sense of forgiveness, comfort and inner peace. "Take part" is an accurate description because the participants sing and recite and read. They do not just sit and listen —sometimes they stand, sometimes kneel. Those who conduct their services wear peculiar uniforms that are also decorated with symbols and have special meaning. In addition, the church has other kinds of services, services related to life's special times—a new baby in the family, a marriage, the death of a loved one. And to some extent those who take part in the ongoing life of the Church carry over its influence and its message into their everyday pursuits.

What is the meaning of all of this? Why is the Christian Church the way it is in looks and in worship, in belief and witness?

Episcopalians, as well as other Christian bodies, think of themselves as the *Family of God*. How do you get acquainted with a family, any family? Perhaps you are invited into the family's home, or you may just wander in because you are lost and have no home of your own. That home is decorated in their special way—there are pictures treasured by the family and little things here and there which have particular meaning for family members. You see that its members have different roles in the life of the family. Their jobs are different as are their responsibilities. You notice that family members have customs and practices peculiarly their own—they hold hands to say grace at meals, or the kids always whistle when they come home from school and enter the house. You find out that there are certain days and occasions which have family importance. When you begin to inquire about family practices they are likely to begin to tell you some family history. "Grandpa was this kind of man and we try to live up to our past." Now you have begun to discover what the members of that family really believe, what it important to them—deep down. If you are an orphan and have no family, perhaps you are attracted to this family you have discovered and would like to be a part of it.

In the following pages we are going to try to tell you those same things about that part of the Family of God known as the Episcopal Church or to use its historical and legal name, The Protestant Episcopal Church in the United States of America. We shall look at its building, its worship, its ministry, its history, and its beliefs. Then we shall describe how a person becomes a member, and what difference that can make in his or her life.

Chapter 2

The House of God

The name "church" has a long history. In time, it came to mean "the house of the Lord" or God's house. And another word came to be associated with the people who worshiped in God's house—the Greek word *ecclesia,* from which we get ecclesiastic. *Ecclesia,* means, literally, "the called out assemble of people," and "those who are called to assemble" (as by the town crier) in the Lord's Name. So "church" has come to mean both God's *house* and God's *people.*

Usually, the architecture of the building adds to our awareness that it is a place of Christian worship. There is a cross on the building and some sort of spire which raises our eyes toward heaven. It may have gothic arches which also point upward, and a tower that tells of God's protection of his people.

Even the position of the building on the lot has Christian significance. From ancient time, churches have been built with the altar at the east end so that the worshipers would be facing the rising sun, symbolic of the Lord's resurrection from the dead. This continues to be a practice even today; the National Cathedral in Washington, D.C., is an example of an eastward orientation. Also, the east is thought of as the direction from which Jesus shall come on the last day. "For as the lightening comes out of the east and shines as far as the west, so will be the coming of the Son of Man" (Matthew 24:27). For this reason, it was once a custom in Christian burial grounds to lay the dead to rest with faces toward the east.

The church building as God's home has been especially set apart for worship. This "setting apart" is called consecrating or dedicating, and takes place in a service performed by the bishop. A consecrated church building is used as a place to worship God and for no other purpose. In the consecration service, the building is given a Christian name. It may be named for our Lord or one of the apostles or saints—Christ Church . . . St. Matthew's Church . . . or St. Patrick's Church—or it may be named for a great doctrine of the Christian faith —the Church of the Incarnation . . . Holy Trinity Episcopal Church.

There is a variety of kinds of churches. Within the Episcopal Church, the principal church of the diocese where the bishop has his official seat or throne (a symbol of his authority) is called a cathedral. (The Greek word *cathedra* means seat or throne.) Most churches where the people of the community worship are called parish churches. In earlier times the parish was a geographic area within which the people lived who worshiped at the local church. This is less true today because people have greater mobility. Also, there are smaller churches called "missions" which have been started by a parish or the diocese, but which are not yet self-supporting.

In addition to the Episcopal churches of the community there are a number of other churches where Christian people worship—Baptist, Methodist, Roman Catholic, Presbyterian, Greek Orthodox to name only a few.

There are also non-Christian places of worship—Jewish synagogues, Islamic mosques.

Now let's open the door and step inside that church on the corner.

Chapter 3

The House Within

The interior of the building is divided into several parts. First there is the porch or vestibule or narthex. Then there is the main body of the church called the nave. This is occupied by those who assemble to worship God. The name nave comes from the Latin word *navis,* meaning ship. The church is the ship of salvation which bears us safely over the stormy seas of life.

Some churches are cruciform, that is, built in the form of a cross, with two transepts, one extending north, the other south, at the head of the aisle.

The front part of the church beyond the transepts is raised a few steps above the nave and is called the chancel. Sometimes it is separated from the nave by an open screen (Latin *cancelli,* hence the name chancel) which, nowadays, is called the rood screen because it is surmounted by a cross or rood. The front part of the chancel is called the choir simply because those who lead the singing sit there. Finally, at the east end of the building behind the chancel rail is the raised and most prominent part of the building, the sanctuary.

Many modern churches are circular with the sanctuary in the middle of the congregation and the choir off to one side. However, regardless of the pattern of the building—cruciform, rectangular, or round—every church has an entrance way, a nave, and a sanctuary, and each section has its own appropriate furnishings.

In many churches the baptismal font is the first thing one sees upon entering the west door. This is a reminder that everyone enters the fellowship of believers through the sacrament of Holy Baptism. That is when "God adopts us as his children and makes us members of Christ's Body, the Church, and inheritors of the kingdom of God" (BCP*, pg. 858). Sometimes, the font is in the front part of the nave. This is partly for practical reasons —so members of the congregation can see and hear better what takes place when one is baptized, and partly for symbolic reasons—font and altar are both placed prominently because they remind us of the two sacraments instituted by our Lord as necessary to salvation.

In many churches there is a Litany desk at the head of the center aisle. At this prayer desk the Litany is said. Its position reminds us that the Litany (BCP, pg. 148) was originally said or sung while walking in procession with the officiating minister in front. Singing the Litany in procession is still the regular practice at the National Cathedral in Washington, D.C., and a number of other churches, as well. The Litany desk is often removed when not in use.

There are two prominent pieces of furniture at the front, in or near the chancel. One is the lectern—the reading stand on which rests the Holy Bible (the name "lectern" comes from the Latin word for reading). The lectern is sometimes in the form of an eagle, a symbol of inspiration and representing the flight of the Gospel

---

*Here, and in the remainder of this book, BCP refers to The Book of Common Prayer, 1979.

throughout the world. The other is the pulpit, a raised platform from which the minister preaches the Word of God and applies its meaning to the lives of hearers. In the Holy Eucharist, the sermon follows the reading of the Gospel and is intended to be an explanation of its meaning. From this ancient practice comes the expression "preaching the Gospel."

The choir stalls or seats as well as those of the participating clergy are in the front of the chancel.

The most prominent object in a church is the altar upon which the Holy Communion part of the Holy Eucharist is celebrated. The altar is also called the Lord's Table, the Holy Table, or simply the Table (BCP, pgs. 341, 361, 573, 574). In some churches, the altar is made of marble. In others, it is made of wood and may really be a table. Several steps lead up to it from the nave and it is guarded by a railing called variously the chancel rail, altar rail, or communion rail.

Back of the altar there is a shelf upon which the altar cross and other ornaments stand. This is the retable or gradin. The little box-like compartment which is built into the retable of many altars is the tabernacle in which the sacrament is kept for the purpose of administering to the sick.

The carved screen of wood or stone which rises behind and above the altar is the reredos. *Reredos* means *back*. A curtain or dossal, or sometimes a painting, replaces it in many churches.

The altar has not always stood against the east wall of the church. At one time it sat permanently in the middle of the nave. Later, because the Holy Table was not being treated with proper respect, it was placed against the east wall and a rail was added to protect it from desecration. Before the American Revolution, lectern and pulpit were often in another part of the building, usually along the north wall, and only the Holy Table and chairs for the clergy were enclosed within the altar rail. After the Revolution, more and more churches had altar, lectern, and pulpit grouped together at the east end of the building. In the middle 1800's, the chancel arrangement of many present-day churches came into vogue. The revived liturgical interest of recent decades has had as one of its results the moving of the altar to a freestanding position in the chancel so that the priest can celebrate the Eucharist facing the people.

The cross that stands on the retable reminds us of our Lord's death and resurrection—his sacrifice for us and for the sin of the whole world, and his rising again whereby we have victory over sin and death. It is this "blessed passion and precious death," this "mighty resurrection and glorious ascension" that we commemorate and celebrate at every Eucharist. In many churches, candles are placed on either side of the cross in order to beautify the sanctuary. In earlier times, the primary reason for a candle or candles on the altar was in order that the celebrant could see. Gaslight and electricity came much later. There continue to be candles on the altar today, because what started out as an aid to physical seeing has now become an aid to the eyes of our minds, helping us to see more in the service. The lighted candles remind us that Jesus Christ is the "Light of the world" (John 8:12). He is "the true light that enlightens everyone" who "believes in him" (John 1:4-12). The lighted candles signify also the joy and splendor that are ours because of the light of the Gospel of Christ. The number of candles varies in different churches and in accordance with the importance of the occasion. A sanctuary lamp burning before the altar indicates that the Blessed Sacrament is reserved.

Flowers also beautify the sanctuary. We take for granted this use of living beauty from God's world of nature as a most natural way to enhance the beauty of our celebration, but this practice has not always been acceptable. At one time, it was considered a sacrilege to place anything around the altar which was not associated with the celebration of the Eucharist. Fortunately, that prohibition has passed. Now there is hardly a church large or small that does not add to the grandeur of the celebration of the Lord's Supper with the beauty of flowers, lovingly-arranged.

It is customary also to adorn the altar with beautiful hangings of silk and other rich material. These hangings have varied considerably through the centuries. In colonial times in this country, for example, the Holy Table was covered with a red or green "carpet" of silk or some other expensive material (although in some churches the material was felt) which extended down to the floor on all sides. During the penitential seasons of Advent and Lent, however, the Table in some churches was completely bare. When there was a celebration of the Holy Communion a white linen tablecloth, reaching almost to the floor, was put over the usual covering. In the latter part of the 1800's the "new" custom of using seasonal colors began, first in a few, then in most, and by 1920 in almost all American churches. These hangings are of colors that convey something of the mood of the various seasons of the Church Year and are embroidered with a variety of Christian emblems. The large hanging which covers the front of the altar is the frontal, and the shorter one which hangs over it is the frontlet or super-frontal.

Chapter 4

Symbolism

The Church has a language of symbols or signs. We experience the language of symbols every day. For example, when we see a yellow road sign with a large plus mark on it we know we are approaching an intersection. Christian symbols remind us of great Christian truths. They are used to decorate and beautify the House of God. The following are a few examples of symbols:

Cross—The most important of all Christian symbols is the cross that reminds us of our Lord's death on Calvary. It was traced on our foreheads in baptism in token that we were "sealed by the Holy Spirit . . . and marked as Christ's own forever." To sign one's self with the sign of the cross is both an act of devotion and a profession of faith. This symbol has many forms. Here are a few of them.

14

Latin cross: This is the cross of western Christendom.

Greek cross: The four equal arms of this cross suggest the Church's mission to the four corners of the world to every race, nation, and class of people.

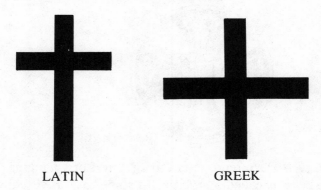

LATIN   GREEK

Maltese cross: This cross was worn by the Knights of St. John or Knights Hospitallers of Malta as early as the eleventh century.

St. Andrew's cross: St. Andrew is said to have died on this kind of cross.

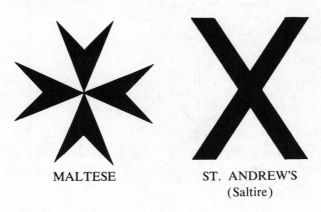

MALTESE   ST. ANDREW'S
                 (Saltire)

Canterbury cross: This cross is a copy of one made perhaps in Kent in the eighth century. Derived from the Alisee Patee, it appears on the coat of arms of the Archbishop of Canterbury.

CANTERBURY

Crucifix: A representation of our Lord hanging on the cross is called a crucifix. In some cases he is shown clothed in royal garments—Christ the king or *Christus Rex* who reigns in glory. The figure, however, is most often depicted in the attitude of suffering.

CHRIST THE KING
CRUCIFIX
(Christus Rex)

Presiding Bishop's cross: The distinctive cross of the Presiding Bishop of the Episcopal Church is pictured on the opposite page.

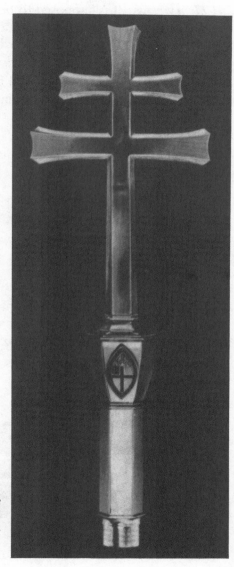

Head of the Primate's Staff of the Presiding Bishop of the Episcopal Church.

Calvary cross: It is supposed to be the actual form of the cross on which our Lord was crucified. The base symbolizes the hill of Calvary on which the crucifixion took place.

Celtic cross: This cross was used by the Celtic Christians of Britain, Scotland, and Ireland. It is called also the Ionic cross.

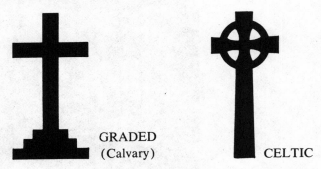

GRADED
(Calvary)

CELTIC

Eastern cross: The upper bar on this cross is for the inscription I.N.R.I. The lower one represents the footrest. It is used in Eastern Orthodox Churches.

Jerusalem cross: This cross was the emblem of the crusaders.

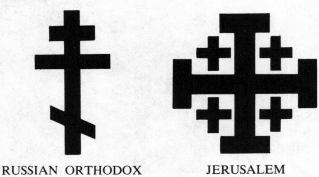

RUSSIAN ORTHODOX   JERUSALEM

Fish—The fish is one of the oldest Christian symbols. Jesus used the fish in his parable of the net to represent those who were gathered into his kingdom. In another sense it represents Christ himself because the initials of the words which compose the Greek phrase, "Jesus Christ Son of God, Savior," spell the Greek word for fish, which is *Icthus.* In ancient times of persecution, this anagram or the figure of a fish became a sort of password or sign by which Christians recognized one another.

Dove—The Holy Spirit is most commonly represented by a dove. This symbol comes from the gospel account of Jesus' baptism. "When Jesus came up out of the water, immediately he saw the heavens opened and the Spirit descending upon him like a dove . . ." (Mark 1:10).

Pelican—There is a legend that the pelican pierces her own breast to feed her young. This symbol represents Christ redeeming the world with his blood and is known as "the pelican in her piety."

Agnus Dei—These Latin words mean "Lamb of God," referring to Jesus. "The next day John the Baptist saw Jesus coming toward him and said, 'Behold, the Lamb of God, who takes away the sin of the word!' " (John 1:29)

IHS—These are the first three letters of the word Jesus in Greek.

XP—Here are the first letters of the Greek word for Christ. The Greek X (chi) is the same as the English CH; the Greek P(rho) is the same as the English R.

A Ω—The Greek letters alpha and omega are the first and last letters of the Greek alphabet, and are a symbol for God. " 'I am the Alpha and the Omega,' says the Lord God, who is and who was and who is to come, the Almighty" (Revelation 1:8).

The Holy Trinity—The triangle, the three-leafed-clover, the fleur-de-lis, three interlocking circles, and other three-fold designs, all symbolize the three persons of the Trinity—Father, Son, and Holy Spirit.

There are many other Christian symbols, but these are among the most common and will help people understand the meaning behind many of the decorations in church.

Chapter 5

The Symbolism of Worship

Symbolism is not just used to decorate our churches. It is used also as a vehicle of worship—a graphic way of setting forth the truth inherent in Christian worship. Symbolism helps to make worship visual and dramatic and, when the symbol used is understood, more intelligible. Here are some of those symbols:

Water—Water calls to mind so many things—washing, refreshment, even life. Among the many references to it in the Bible are the following: The creation story begins with water: ". . . the Spirit of God was moving over the face of the waters . . ." (Genesis 1:2). Water calls to mind "the Father Almighty, creator of heaven and earth." Later, God led the Children of Israel through the waters of the Red Sea to freedom from Egyptian bondage. Not only is God the Creator, but he cares, delivers, saves. God saved the lives of the Israelites in the wilderness by giving them water to drink (Exodus 15:22-27). The saving power of God with water as the vehicle moves from the physical to the spiritual level in the New Testament. Jesus was baptized by John in the waters of the Jordan River and "was anointed by the Holy Spirit as the Messiah" (Mark 1:9-11). After Jesus' crucifixion and resurrection people were received into the company of believers by a baptism which dramatized the death and resurrection experience of the candidates. They went down under the water (a watery grave) and came up again (resurrection) new creatures blessed with the Holy Spirit. So the Christian's faith in the crucified and risen Lord is tied up with the symbolism of water. (See the "Thanksgiving over the Water" in the Baptismal Service, BCP, pg. 306.) Water is used also by Christians as a symbol for cleansing, to typify the purification of persons or objects that are blessed by the Church. The use of blessed or consecrated water—holy water—is an old and widespread Christian custom.

Bread and wine—In the Holy Eucharist, bread and wine represent the body and blood of Christ. The bread broken and the wine poured out symbolize his death on the cross. These elements—bread and wine—are symbols of spiritual nourishment. The Holy Communion is a heavenly banquet—"the bread of heaven" and "the cup of salvation" as the Prayer Book puts it (BCP, pgs. 338 and 365). Our spiritual lives are sustained and nourished by the Lord's life and spirit. The Prayer Book puts the deeper meaning of being fed with God's "gifts and creatures of bread and wine" in these words: ". . . that we, receiving them according to thy Son our Savior Jesus Christ's holy institution, in remembrance of his death and passion, may be partakers of his most blessed Body and Blood" (BCP, pg. 335).

Laying on of hands—There is a warmth and a sustaining quality to the human touch. The touch of sympathy when words fail and the pat on the back of encouragement or congratulations are familiar to all. In Christian worship the laying on of hands is a recognized way to transmit power or blessing. The context and the accompanying words interpret the act. The bishop or the priest lays a hand on the person's head and marks his forehead with the sign of the cross in Baptism. The bishop lays hands on the head of a person in Confirmation. So also in ordination to all three orders of the ordained ministry —deacons, priests, and bishops—hands are laid on the candidate's head. The priest lays a hand upon the penitent's head in the course of the Reconciliation of a Penitent (BCP, pg. 451) and also in the course of prayer for a sick person (BCP, pg. 455). This is a time-honored symbol of transmitting spiritual power which is repeatedly mentioned in the Old and New Testaments. Here are a few of them: Mark 5:23, 6:5; Acts 6:6; 8:17f; 9:17; 13:3; 19:6; 1 Timothy 4:14; 5:22; 2 Timothy 1:6; Hebrews 6:2.

Incense—When incense is used in Christian worship it creates the aura of holiness which is associated with divinity. That is why frankincense was appropriately one of the gifts the Magi brought to the Christ Child. Sometimes it symbolizes the rising petitions of prayer and sometimes it is used in the hallowing of persons or things. The use of incense in worship had great significance in the Old Testament. Early Christians avoided its use because it was associated with pagan cults and emperor-worship, but it has been used in worship by some branches of Christendom since the fourth century.

Ashes—Ashes symbolize penitence. At one time all devout Christians were signed with ashes on their foreheads on the first day of Lent. That is how Ash Wednesday got its name. The custom is still followed in many churches.

Color symbolism—The traditional liturgical colors have this symbolism: white for rejoicing, red for fire and for the blood of the martyrs; violet for penitence; green for the color of nature; and black for mourning. These colors are used to convey the feeling or mood of the days, and seasons of the Church Year and of special occasions and in the celebration of certain rites and sacraments. The usual occasions for their use are:

White: On the great festivals of Christmas and Easter, on the feasts of our Lord, All Saints' Day and saints' days which do not commemorate martyrdoms, and at marriages.

Red: On Pentecost and on the days commemorating martyred saints, also at ordinations and sometimes for Confirmation.

Violet: In Advent and Lent, and on Rogation and Ember Days.

Black: On Good Friday.

Green: All Sundays after Epiphany and on the Sundays of Pentecost following Trinity Sunday.

(Although violet or even black is used sometimes at burials, white is more appropriate because of the resurrection theme of the service.)

Vestments—Another aspect of the symbolism of worship is the vestments which are worn while conducting the services. The first vestments in western Christendom (the origin of our present vestments) were usually the formal secular dress of the Roman Empire of the early centuries of the Christian era. The alb, described below, is the only exception. In time there were garments specifically designed for liturgical use as distinct from the reservation on one's "best clothes" for such a purpose. One of the Roman emperors criticized the Christians of his day because they dressed up in special clothes to worship God. As the use of vestments continued there was the tendency to try to find a Biblical rationale for everything connected with worship (especially the Eucharist) in terms of details of the passion, and to interpret vestments in terms of a symbolism of virtues and graces.

We are thankful for this development in the long life of the Church because this special church clothing serves several useful purposes. (1) It must be beautiful for it is the very essence of worship that it should reflect and acknowledge the beauty of God as revealed in his mighty acts of creation and redemption. (2) It serves a historical and theological function. The vestments are ancient in origin and reflect the continuity of Christian worship through the ages. In addition, their ornamentation has made them vehicles for proclaiming aspects of Christian belief. (3) Finally, vestments are functional. They enable people to be able to distinguish the roles and ranks of each participant. For these reasons they are an important part of the symbolism of worship.

The Priest's Eucharistic Vestments consist of the following:

Cassock: It is a long (usually) black garment which reaches to the feet and symbolizes service. It is worn by all three orders of ordained clergy.

Alb: This is a long white garment with narrow sleeves which is worn over the cassock. It is appropriate as a symbol of purity and wholeness acquired by the Christian in baptism.

Amice: This is a broad band of white material, sometimes ornamented with embroidery, which is worn about the neck. It was originally a protection for the head and neck against the cold; afterward it came to symbolize the helmet of salvation.

Girdle: This is the white rope worn around the waist. It is sometimes said to symbolize temperance and chastity, sometimes, being girded with truth (Ephesians 6:14).

Maniple: Originally this was a towel or napkin and symbolizes the humility which befits a servant of God.

Stole: This is a long narrow scarf, usually of silk, which hangs about the shoulders and symbolizes the yoke of service. Its color is usually that of the church season, and the ends are embroidered with appropriate symbols. It is the insignia of priesthood.

Chasuble: It is a large garment which is put over the head, and hangs down before and behind. Both back and front may be marked with Y-shaped crosses or orphreys. The orphrey in front is sometimes a single strip or pillar and is said to represent the column or pillar to which our Lord was bound. This vestment may be white or the color of the season and it is frequently ornamented with embroideries. It is said to represent the seamless coat with which our Lord was clothed and signifies love.

In some parishes the priest wears a surplice and stole for celebrating the Holy Eucharist instead of eucharistic vestments.

Surplice: This is a flowing vestment of white material which is worn over the cassock. It is a modified version of the alb and, like the alb, reminds us of the purity of life which should characterize those who minister in the sanctuary.

Tippet: At services when the stole is not used this wide black scarf is worn around the neck with the ends pendant in front. Some form of it was originally an academic vestment.

Hood: College and university graduates wear hoods of silk or other fine material thrown back over their shoulders. The shape and color indicate the degree received and the institution granting it.

Biretta and Canterbury Cap: These are clergy hats that may be worn at open air services, in draughty church buildings, or in procession. Neither is ever worn in the sanctuary.

Cope: This is a long ornate cloak worn by a priest or a bishop in processions and services of great dignity.

Bishop's Vestments: Over his cassock the bishop wears a long white garment with very full "bishop's" sleeves called a *rochet;* and over this a sleeveless vestment of black or purple or red silk or satin, called a *chimere.* About his shoulders he wears a tippet or stole and he may also wear an academic hood. Sometimes in place of the foregoing he may wear a cope and a head covering called a *mitre.* The latter is a high silk cap, terminating in two points, which are said to symbolize the tongues of fire which lighted upon the heads of the apostles at Pentecost (Acts 2:3). He carries in his hand, or has carried before him, the *pastoral staff* or shepherd's crook which signified that he is the chief shepherd of his people. The rest of the Episcopal insignia consists of a *pectoral cross* and a *seal ring* engraved with the arms of the diocese. The ring signifies his lifelong marriage to the Church.

Deacon's Vestments: The deacon wears the same cassock, surplice, and stole as a priest. His ordained rank is indicated by the way he or she wears the stole. It is only over the left shoulder, signifying that the full rank of priesthood has not yet been attained.

Vestments of the Laity: Lay assistants in the chancel and choristers also wear appropriate vestments. Men and boys wear the cassock and a short surplice called a *cotta.* Women usually wear academic gowns or short white cloaks with collars over a long black garment similar to a cassock. On their heads they may wear caps or veils.

Chapter 6

The Worship of the Church—
The Book of Common Prayer

The pattern of prayer and praise normally used in the worship of Almighty God is set forth in the Book of Common Prayer, commonly called the Prayer Book. The term "common prayer" describes a characteristic of worship in the Episcopal Church. Those who assemble have in common a responsibility to participate. The priest or minister at the front has his or her special role but this becomes a hollow performance apart from the active participation of the others who are present. The assembly is a congregation—people who have come together or congregated to worship God. The services are not a spectator sport where people gather to watch others perform. There is no audience. Someone once said that when a person comes to church he finds himself sitting on the stage—an active participant—not sitting in the audience watching. All of us take part in *common* prayer.

One graphic indication of the fact that common participation is a hallmark of Prayer Book services is the presence of rubrics on almost every page. The rubrics are the italicized fine print directions which instruct participants as to how to proceed. They are called "rubrics" because they are sometimes printed in red, as in the large altar book used by the priest. (*Ruber* is the

Latin word for red.) There is also a page at the beginning
of each service entitled "Concerning the Service," and a
section of "Additional Directions" follows most of the
services in the book (BCP, pgs. 312 and 406 are examples.) These together provide all of the directions needed
for conducting and participating in Prayer Book services.
The priest or minister does not have any secret book of
mysterious things he does which those attending do not
understand. We all have the same book; it is truly common prayer.

When we open the book we discover that it contains
services and rites for regular worship as well as those
that appropriate for the milestone events of every individual Christian—baptism through burial. The contents
are made up of passages of Scripture as well as prayers
and hymns and rituals many of which have been part of
Christian practice from the earliest times. It contains
also the entire Book of Psalms from the Bible.

The first Book of Common Prayer was compiled under
the leadership of Archbishop Thomas Cranmer in 1549.
Down through the centuries, first in England, then in
this country, the Prayer Book has been revised eight
times. The most recent American revision is that adopted
by the General Convention in 1979. The Prayer Book
was revised because times change and the spiritual needs
of the new day must be met. The meanings of words
change and some prayers have to be rephrased in order
to convey their ancient meaning. Also, scholars acquire
new and greater knowledge about the early Church and
its life and practice which should be reflected in our
worship. But every revision of the Prayer Book has
measured up to the three criteria which Archbishop
Cranmer laid down for the first Prayer Book back in

1549. The book must be "grounded upon the Holy Scriptures," "agreeable to the order of the primitive church," and "edifying to the people." So each succeeding revision, while having its own distinctive character, has been in spirit and truth the same Book of Common Prayer.

The services of the Book of Common Prayer fall into four categories. There are the regular services—the Holy Eucharist which is intended to be celebrated every Sunday and on holy days, and Morning and Evening Prayer, known as the Daily Offices, which are intended to be used every day of the week as well as on Sunday.

A second category is services for special days. The Great Litany is especially appropriate during Lent, on the Rogation Days, and on the First Sunday in Advent. There are liturgies for Ash Wednesday, Holy Week, and the vigil which ushers in Easter Day. These occasions are milestones in the Church's calendar and these special services take note of that fact.

A third category of services is those used for personal milestone occasions. These cover the whole gambit of human experience—Baptism, Confirmation, Commitment to Christian Service, Marriage, Thanksgiving for the Birth or Adoption of a Child, Reconciliation of a Penitent, Ministration to the Sick and Dying, and Burial. All of these services are related to happenings in the lives of people.

There is still a fourth category of services—those performed by a bishop. These are the Episcopal Services. They include the Making or Ordaining of a Bishop, Priest, or Deacon, Celebration of a New Ministry, and Consecration of a Church or Chapel.

The Prayer Book, then, contains the material which assists us in holding up to God the whole of our lives and the extent of our days. It preserves for us the ways in which the people of God have done this through long generations. It is indeed a precious heritage.

The other book in the pews of every Episcopal Church is The Hymnal. It has not had so long and constant a history as the Prayer Book. In the first American Prayer Book, for example, the words to 27 hymns were printed at the end of the book, but there was no music. Since then, there have been six revisions and enlargements, the last being in 1982—the book which is now in use. The 720 hymns in the present book cover a wide spectrum of our Christian heritage. The poems come from almost every century of our Christian past and from poets who have diverse Christian backgrounds. This richness of variety is also found in the tunes. The Catholic Church of the ages in its breadth and richness is present in our hymnal.

Now, let's examine the Prayer Book services in some detail and seek to appreciate their meaning.

Chapter 7

The Worship of the Church—
Morning and Evening Prayer

Morning and Evening Prayer have ancient roots which go back to the synagogue services of the Old Testament. Their immediate predecessor is the hour services of the monasteries of the Middle Ages. In compiling our first Book of Common Prayer three of the morning hour services—Matins, Lauds, and Prime—were, in a sense, telescoped into what that book called Matins. It is now known more commonly as Morning Prayer. In like manner, two evening services—Vespers and Compline—were combined to become Evensong or Evening Prayer. The intention and spirit of the hour services might be summed up by the verse, "Seven times a day do I praise thee." The first English Prayer Book was published at a time when reading the Bible in understandable English (rather than in ancient Latin) was new, exciting, and edifying. We can, therefore, see why the verse, "Thy Word is a lantern unto my feet," more nearly captures the spirit of the new services of Morning and Evening Prayer. Whether it was the intention of the compilers of the first Prayer Book or not, these Daily Offices gained a prominence in practice which eclipsed the Sacrament of the Lord's Supper as the chief Sunday service. Subsequent revisions of the Prayer Book in England for more than one hundred years further encouraged this custom.

About 150 years ago, a small group at Oxford University, England, started a movement which focused attention on the practices of the Church during the early centuries. The effects of that Oxford Movement have influenced profoundly the worship of the Church in this country as well as in England, and one result is that the Lord's Supper is increasingly becoming the principal Sunday service. However, there are still many churches in which Morning Prayer is the principal service on several Sundays each month.

Both Morning and Evening Prayer have as their central focus the reading of the Word of God. They both follow the same three-part pattern—like a play in three acts.

Act One: The opening sentences (BCP, pgs. 37-40 and 75-78) make us realize that we have come into God's presence. These sentences will vary according to the occasion or the season. From them we catch something of the quality and spirit of this encounter with the Almighty. Our awareness of the greatness and glory of the Lord our God makes us realize how far short we fall of being worthy to be called his faithful servants. So we fall on our knees and confess our sins (BCP, pg. 41 and 79). Then, through the priest, we receive absolution—the merciful Lord does forgive those who are penitent (I John 1:8-9). So ends the first act of the drama. We are now ready to hear God's Word.

Act Two: "O Lord, open thou our lips and our mouth shall show forth thy praise" (BCP, pg. 42 and 80). This is our joyful response to the forgiveness we have just received, and the Psalm and the canticles throughout this part of the service continue this note of thanksgiving and praise. It is in this joyful and warm atmosphere that we now hear readings from the Word of God. Following this Biblical instruction, we stand and confess our faith in the words of the Apostles' Creed. Often it has some new overtones of meaning because of the Scripture we have just heard. Also, the message of that Scripture is enhanced by hearing it alongside of the Creed's summary of the whole of our Christian belief. With this, the instruction and praise of Act Two come to a close.

Act Three: We have met the Lord and experienced his forgiveness. We have heard his Word and discovered new meaning in it for our lives. Now we bring our petitions and intercessions to God (BCP, pg. 54ff and 97ff). In the course of this closer communion we pray for ourselves in our various ministries, for the civil authorities, and for the Church—its clergy, its people, its mission, and for those with special needs, such as sorrow or affliction. Finally, we pray that we may have the grace to transform this moment of prayer and praise into faithful living—"that we may show forth thy praise, not only with our lips, but in our lives" (BCP, pg. 59 and 101). On this resolute note the Third Act closes.

How used: Morning and Evening Prayer may be used in full or they may be abbreviated in accordance with the provisions of the rubrics. Either service may be substituted for the Word of God portion of the Holy Eucharist. When used on Sunday without the Eucharist, Morning Prayer invariably includes a sermon and a dismissal or blessing. The sermon may follow the Scripture readings or follow a hymn at the conclusion of the Office or come after the collects (rubric, BCP, pg. 142). These services may be rendered either in an ordinary tone of voice or sung. Evening Prayer or Evensong is most frequently sung.

Chapter 8

The Worship of the Church—
The Holy Eucharist

The Holy Eucharist was instituted by our Lord Jesus Christ at the Last Supper as a memorial of the sacrifice which he was about to make on the cross, and as a regular means through which we ourselves become sharers in that sacrifice and participate in its benefits. (Another way in which we share in his death and resurrection is Holy Baptism, see Chapter 20). It is the only service of worship that our Lord instituted and is, therefore, more important than any other. As the Lord's own service it is or ought to be the principal service on the Lord's Day.

Various names have been given this service to express its different features and emphases. Because our Lord gave thanks when he broke the bread, the early Christians called it the *Holy Eucharist* (*eucharist* means *thanks*). That note of thanksgiving runs all through the Holy Communion portion of the service. The name *Holy Communion* (*communion* means *sharing*) derives from the fact that when we receive God's gifts of bread and wine according to Christ's holy institution and in remembrance of his death and passion, we are "partakers of his most blessed Body and Blood" (BCP, pg. 335). The service is called, also, the *Lord's Supper* for obvious reasons, the *Mass* which is probably a corruption of the

Latin word for the dismissal, and, in the Greek Orthodox Church, the *Divine Liturgy.*

Morning and Evening Prayer are sometimes called choir offices because they are said by the minister in the choir outside the chancel rail. In the Eucharist, the Holy Communion portion of the service is celebrated at the altar—"the service of the altar." The choir offices may be conducted by a deacon or a layreader, as is also true of the Word of God portion of the Holy Eucharist, but the Holy Communion can be celebrated only by a priest or a bishop.

The basic meaning of the Holy Eucharist is that of a heavenly meal—"the foretaste of the heavenly banquet which is our nourishment in eternal life" (BCP, pg. 860). Just as physical food strengthens and refreshes our bodies so the life and Spirit of the risen Christ—his Body and Blood—cloaked in the consecrated bread and wine strengthen and refresh our souls.

The Prayer Book makes it quite clear that the service of the Holy Eucharist has two major divisions, like a drama in two acts—The Word of God (BCP, pgs. 323 and 355) and The Holy Communion (BCP, pgs. 333 and 361). During the Word of God part of the service the action takes place around the lectern and the pulpit; during the Holy Communion the altar is central. During that first act hearing and learning are the characteristics of those taking part; during the second act giving and responding set the tone of the action.

Act One: The Word of God. The service begins with the opening acclamation appropriate to the season or occasion, followed by the Collect for Purity that we may be worthy to "magnify thy holy Name." The *Gloria in excelsis,* a very ancient hymn of praise, anticipates the joyful spirit with which the whole service will be infused and from which it takes its name—the Holy Eucharist. The Collect of the Day puts something of this day's meaning in a prayer that God will give us grace to live by its light. (See the Sunday Collects, BCP pgs. 159-185 and 211-236.) Then the Lessons are read—Old Testament, Epistle, and Gospel—and a portion of the Psalter. These constitute the Word of God to us on this day. After each of the first two readings provision is made for a few moments of silence so that we, who are worshiping, may have the opportunity to let God speak to our hearts. After the Gospel comes the sermon to enlighten us as to its meaning for us and our times. The Nicene Creed sets forth the whole tapestry of Christian belief against which we now see the special teaching for this day as a part.

The Prayers of the People (BCP, pgs. 328 and 383ff) hold up to God the needs of the Church and the world, as well as the special needs of individuals and groups known to those taking part in the service. The new insights each worshiper has gained from the hearing of God's Word set Christian responsibility and concern in new perspective.

Then follows the Confession of Sin, the Absolution, and the Comfortable Words. The worshipers realize how far short they come of being the Lord's loyal and faithful servants. This awareness and God's forgiveness are an important part of our preparation to share in the Holy Communion which follows. The Penitential Order (BCP, pgs. 319 and 351) may be used at the beginning of the service as the act of preparation for participation in the whole rite in place of the Confession of Sin at this point in the service.

Peace with God, growing out of our confession of sin and being absolved, issues in reconciliation with our neighbors: we greet one another in the Lord's Name (the Peace, BCP, pgs. 332 and 360). This important liturgical act is a scripturally sound transition to the Offertory: "First be reconciled to your brother, and then come and offer your gift" (Matthew 5:24). On this note the first act of the drama closes.

It is permissible to substitute Morning or Evening Prayer for the Word of God portion of the Holy Eucharist (rubric, BCP, pg. 322). Note that when the Penitential Order (BCP, pg. 319) is used at the beginning of the service in place of the Confession of Sin the sequence of the service is almost exactly like that of Morning or Evening Prayer.

The second act of the drama of the Holy Eucharist is called the Holy Communion. In previous editions of the Book of Common Prayer the name Holy Communion was used as the title of the whole service. Now the more ancient title—the Holy Eucharist—is used for the entire service and Holy Communion is applied only to that portion of the service in which worshipers commune.

Act Two: The Holy Communion. The Offertory is a dramatic offering to God of our alms and the oblations of bread and wine. These are highly symbolic gifts. Our alms are those monies we have received for our creative endeavors. A person's money is all he has to show as a result of days and hours of working at his trade or business. The amount he gives, therefore, represents that portion of his creative existence that he gives to the Church for use in the Lord's work. (This is more fully explained on page 127.) The bread and wine are gifts of God—wheat and grapes—upon which human ingenuity and skill have been at work in transforming them into the special food and drink they are. In their present form they represent our labor and our leisure. These precious gifts, representing all that we are and all that we treasure, we bring and present at the Lord's altar.

Now comes *the Great Thanksgiving,* the high point of the service. We praise God in the *Sursum Corda* and *Sanctus* (the Latin names for "Lift up your hearts" and the three-fold "Holy") joining voices with "all the company of heaven," especially for the evidence of God's power and glory which we celebrate on this particular day (see the Proper Prefaces which are inserted at every celebration, BCP, pgs. 344-349 and 377-382). This is followed by the *Eucharistic Prayer,* often called the *Prayer of Consecration. Consecrate* means *to set apart for* or *dedicate to* God's holy purposes. In celebrating the Holy Communion the priest first places the bread on a small plate called a *paten,* and the wine is poured into a cup or *chalice.* Then the celebrant prays that our bread and wine be sanctified by God's Holy Spirit "to be for your people the Body and Blood of your Son, the holy food and drink of new and unending life in him" (BCP, pg. 363, similar wording is contained in the other Eucharistic Prayers which may be used in the service). Awareness of the Lord's great sacrifice for us inspires our responding "sacrifice of praise and thanks-giving." We pray that the Holy Spirit will sanctify us also that, having faithfully received this holy Sacrament, we may serve him in unity, constancy, and peace; and at the last day join with all his saints in the joy of his eternal kingdom. The consecrated people are now ready to receive through faith the Body and Blood of the Lord. The Eucharistic Prayer climaxes with the Lord's Prayer.

When we analyze the account of the Last Supper, we see that our Lord did four things. He took bread, blessed it, broke it, and gave it to his people. In the Eucharistic Prayer the celebrant takes bread and blesses it. Now comes what is called *The Fraction* when the bread is broken. A period of silence is kept when the celebrant breaks the consecrated bread so that the worshipers may have an opportunity to meditate. Christ's Body was broken for us; so this breaking calls to mind Jesus' sacrifice on our behalf. We begin to realize anew how great was his love for us—he was willing to die in our behalf.

Now comes the final one of the four eucharistic acts: the "bread of heaven" and "the cup of salvation" are distributed to the people. Then in the closing prayer we thank God "for feeding us with the spiritual food . . . these holy mysteries" and we pray that the Father will "send us out to do the work you have given us to do . . . as faithful witnesses of Christ our Lord" (BCP, pg. 366).

Chapter 9

The Worship of the Church—
Other Services

In addition to the Daily Offices and the Eucharist, the Prayer Book is rich in services for a variety of occasions. When we look at the Table of Contents we find the following headings:

> The Great Litany
> Proper Liturgies for Special Days
> Holy Baptism
> Pastoral Offices
> Episcopal Services

Here, we shall examine the Great Litany, the Proper Liturgies for Special Days and the Episcopal Services. In later chapters, we will take a look at the Pastoral Offices. Holy Baptism will be discussed during our look at the sacraments (Chapter 20).

The Great Litany (BCP, pg. 148). This is a service of responsive prayer which consists of five parts:

1) Invocations–solemn addresses to the Holy Trinity,
2) Deprecations–petitions for deliverance from all evil,
3) Obsecrations–entreaties addressed to the Lord recalling his redeeming acts on our behalf,
4) Suffrages or petitions–chiefly intercessory, ending with renewed invocations to our Lord and the Lord's Prayer, and

5) Concluding prayers–which may include a special Supplication of responsive versicles.

When we looked at the furnishings of the church building we talked about the Litany Desk which stands in the body of the church at the head of the center aisle (Chapter 3). Unless the Litany is sung in procession, it is said with the officient kneeling or standing at the Litany Desk. This service is especially appropriate during Lent and on Rogation Days. In some churches it is used on the First Sunday in Advent. The Great Litany may be used before the Eucharist, as a part of Morning or Evening Prayer, or separately.

Proper Liturgies for Special Days. There are several days throughout the Church Year that deserve to be celebrated in a way peculiar to that day alone. For each of these occasions there is an appropriate liturgy.
**At the service on Ash Wednesday (BCP, pgs. 264-269), the first day of Lent, there is the imposition of ashes. This practice goes back to the Middle Ages and dramatizes the penitent attitude of the individual as he or she enters upon the observance of Lent.
**The Palm Sunday service (BCP, pgs. 270-273) includes the blessing and distribution of palms reminiscent of the Lord's Triumphal Entry into Jerusalem at the beginning of Holy Week (Mark 11:1-11).
**The Maundy Thursday service (BCP, pgs. 274-275) celebrates the institution of the Lord's Supper and John 13 links the ceremony of footwashing with that occasion. The name of the day comes from the Latin for words in our Lord's Upper Room discourse: "A new commandment"—*mandatum* (John 13:34).

**On Good Friday there are meditations on our Lord's passion and death, and appropriate intercessions (BCP, pgs. 276-282).

**Holy Saturday is observed with a brief and awesome remembrance of the day on which the crucified Lord's body was laid in the tomb (BCP, pg. 283).

**On the Great Vigil of Easter (BCP, pgs. 285-295) the transition is made from the somberness of Holy Saturday to the celebration of the glorious resurrection of Christ the Lord—the Pascal Candle is lighted, an elaborate Liturgy of the Word tells the Bible's story of the resurrection, new members are baptized into the Household of God, and worshipers renew their baptismal vows. All this climaxes in the first Easter Day Eucharist celebrating the Day of the Resurrection.

Episcopal Services. The services in this section of the Prayer Book (pgs. 510-579) are related to the special authority and responsibility of bishops. The first three services are for the ordaining or conferring on a bishop, a priest, and a deacon that authority and right to perform the duties of those respective offices or orders of the ministry. There is a further discussion of the ordained ministry in Chapter 21. See also the Catechism for an outline of the duties of each order (BCP, pgs. 855-856).

The Litany for Ordinations is a part of every ordination service. Anyone taking part in an ordination service may be appointed to lead it. That person does not have to be a bishop.

Celebration of a New Ministry is the service appropriate when a new rector is installed in a parish. It is usually conducted by the bishop although he may deputize a priest to act in his stead.

The Dedication and Consecration of a Church is the service the bishop uses in setting a building apart for the worship of Almighty God. We discussed this in Chapter 2.

Chapter 10

The Worship of the Church—
Pastoral Offices

The services described in the previous chapter (with the exception of the Episcopal Services) all have to do with milestone occasions of calendar importance. The Pastoral Offices, found on pages 413 through 507 of the Book of Common Prayer, are services that celebrate milestone events of personal importance. These occasions take place during the whole of one's earthly existence—from birth to death, Baptism through Burial.

Baptism is properly placed alongside the Eucharist in the Prayer Book—the two great sacraments instituted by our Lord—and will be discussed in detail when we deal with the sacraments (Chapter 20).

Confirmation is the rite that marks the occasion when one becomes a responsible member of the Church. It will be discussed when we deal with every person's commitment and responsibilities as a member of the Church (Chapter 23).

The other Pastoral Offices occur in the Prayer Book in the following order:

Commitment to Service. When a person comes to what is for him or her a milestone in his life of service in the world he may want to make the occasion one of Christian rededication. "A Form of Commitment to Christian

Service" is a little public service for this purpose. The individual may have just come to see his employment as an avenue for serving the Lord, or he may be about to start a new job or undertake new responsibilities which he wishes to do as Christ's faithful follower. This service gives concrete expression to the Christian's duty "to work . . . for the spread of the kingdom of God" (BCP, pg. 856).

Celebration and Blessing of a Marriage. The couple who wish to be married in the church and have their marriage blessed must sign a Declaration of Intention. The declaration defines Holy Matrimony as a lifelong union of husband and wife for the purpose of (1) mutual fellowship, encouragement, and understanding, (2) for the procreation (if it may be) of children, and their physical and spiritual nurture, and (3) for the safeguarding and benefit of society. In the course of the service their lifelong vows are symbolized by the ring or rings given and received, and by prayers that God will give them grace "that with true fidelity and steadfast love they may honor and keep" their vows. The Church blesses their serious commitment to live together faithfully until parted by death. The primary reason for being married by a priest in Church is in order to seek God's blessing on the couple as they begin their life together.

The Blessing of a Civil Marriage. Sometimes a couple who have been legally married by a civil authority wish to have the Church's blessing on their marriage. This service provides for that occasion.

An Order of Marriage. Some couples wish to compose their own marriage service or use some form of marriage not found in the Book of Common Prayer. Here are the rubrical requirements with which such a service   must comply in order that it be both legal and acceptable in the Episcopal Church.

A Thanksgiving for the Birth or Adoption of a Child. When a child comes into a family, this is a wonderful and solemn occasion which deserves to be celebrated with joy and thanksgiving and commitment. A child may be born into a family or become a member through legal adoption. In either case it is appropriate to celebrate that important family milestone in God's House.

The Reconciliation of a Penitent. The Prayer Book states: "The Ministry of reconciliation which has been committed by Christ to his Church is exercised through the care each Christian has for others, through the common prayer of Christians assembled for public worship, and *through the priesthood of the Church and its ministers declaring absolution*" (BCP, pg. 446). This latter responsibility (italics mine) has its roots in the occasion when the risen Lord bestowed on the apostles the authority to pronounce in the Name of God the forgiveness of sins of those who are penitent (John 20:22-23). That same authority is vested in every ordained priest. As the Lord's commissioned agent he or she bestows forgiveness on the penitent in God's Name. It is God who really forgives. Every confession, therefore, is to God, whether we make it alone or in the presence of a priest.

Ministration to the Sick. How very often in the Gospels we find Jesus ministering to the sick and suffering—the diseased, the crippled, the blind, and those mentally ill (possessed of demons is the way they described it). The service includes a service of the Word, an opportunity to confess one's sins and be absolved, the laying on of hands and anointing, and Holy Communion. All of it or portions of it may be used with those who are sick, depending on the circumstances. There are not only a number of appropriate prayers from which to choose (BCP, pgs. 458ff), there are also helpful prayers for the sick person to use in his or her private devotions. This part of the Prayer Book has great warmth and relevance. A significant part of this Prayer Book office is the act of anointing with oil or unction of the sick. This rite dates back to the New Testament times (James 5:14-15). The form for this ancient Christian practice (see BCP, pgs. 455-456) consists of anointing with consecrated oil, prayers for the forgiveness of the person's sins and for his or her recovery. When the sick one cannot recover unction is a preparation for death.

Ministration at the Time of Death. When a person is near death his family and loved ones can only watch and wait and pray. This service puts one's deepest thoughts and faith and hope into words. Portions of it may be used depending on the situation.

The Burial of the Dead. This office proclaims the message of Easter, and the family and friends of the departed hear it as applied to themselves and their departed loved one. The service at the church treats the person who has died almost like a guest of honor who is now going forth to serve the Lord in "the land of light and joy in the fellowship of thy saints." During the service the veil between the Church Militant and the Church Triumphant is very thin. After the benediction at the grave the family and friends return to their daily pursuits to serve with a new vision of what their Resurrection faith now means, and with new resolve that "the God of peace, who brought again from the dead our Lord Jesus Christ" work in them "that which is well pleasing in his sight."

Chapter 11

Church Customs and Practices

That which we do in the course of worshiping Almighty God is of a piece with what we say or sing. Our physical behavior is the outward expression of our feelings of reverence and devotion. Church manners are good manners in the presence of the almighty and merciful Father of all. For instance, if one goes to a party or any gathering at a friend's home, it is a matter of good manners to speak to one's host upon entering and to tell him good-bye and thank him for including you before you leave. Any time you enter God's House it is a matter of reverence to kneel and realize where you are and ask God to help you be attentive to the promptings of his Spirit. Then, before you leave, kneel and thank him for the privilege of coming to his House and pray that you may live in the light of the insights you have gained. (See BCP, pgs. 833-834, Nos. 64 and 68 for suggested prayers to use).

Here are some of the other customs and practices of churchgoing people:

Reverent Postures:

(1) *Standing.* We stand to sing God's praise. We stand to affirm our faith when we say the Creed. We stand in reverence at the reading of the Gospel in the Eucharist. He is the Lord of Hosts (literally, ''the commander-in-

chief of the armies'') and the troops stand at attention when the general addresses them. In the Eastern Church it is customary to stand to pray. This practice, which is perfectly permissible in Prayer Book worship, is also followed in many congregations.

(2) *Sitting.* Usually, we sit to learn. So we sit to hear the Word of God read to us. We sit also for the sermon. In some congregations the people sit during the reading of the Psalter.

(3) *Kneeling.* This is the usual posture when praying whether in public or private. Of course, any reverent posture is appropriate when one consciously comes into the presence of Almighty God, but the prevailing sentiment of western Christendom has favored kneeling as the natural expression of reverence when addressing the Heavenly Father. We usually kneel to receive the sacrament, except where the parish custom is to receive standing, and it is quite proper to receive standing if because of age or infirmity one cannot kneel.

Reverent Actions:

(1) *The sign of the Cross.* When we were baptized we were signed on our foreheads with the sign of the cross in token that we "are sealed by the Holy Spirit in Baptism and marked as Christ's own forever." When the bishop or a priest blesses or absolves the congregation, he traces a cross with his uplifted hand. As a token of personal devotion it is appropriate for those present to sign themselves with the sign of the cross. This reverent gesture may give outward expression to our Godward thoughts on innumerable occasions both in church services and elsewhere.

(2) *Bowing*. Many devout worshipers bow their heads at the Name of Jesus whenever it is mentioned, but particularly in the recitation of the Creeds. Christians also bow out of reverence for the cross—the symbol of God's love and of our redemption—when it passes in procession and when they pass before the altar.

(3) *Genuflecting*. It is an act of reverence to genuflect or kneel momentarily upon one knee when approaching or passing before the consecrated Host in devotional recognition of our Lord's presence. It is also proper to bow or genuflect at the words of the Creed, "and was incarnate by the Holy Ghost of the Virgin Mary, and was made man." So we acknowledge the mystery of the Incarnation. .

How to Receive Communion. When we come to the Altar Rail to receive "the holy food and drink of new and unending life in him," the proper things to do are determined by our sense of reverence and consideration. While customs vary from parish to parish, there are two ways in which persons normally receive. The first is by receiving and consuming the Bread and the Wine at the time when they are administered; the second is by intinction. It is proper and reverent to receive the consecrated Host in two hands, one resting upon the other, palms inward. It is considerate as well as reverent to hold the hands level with one's face. The person administering has a paten filled with the consecrated Hosts which are less likely to be spilled if he does not have to bend down to reach your hands; also for your part you are reaching up eagerly for the Bread of life. In some parishes, the priest places the Host on one's tongue. Similar considerateness couples with reverence in receiving the Cup of salvation. One's reverent eagerness is expressed by using both hands to guide the cup to one's lips and away. There is less likelihood of wine being spilled and of disrupting the devotions of those around you when your hands are unmistakably guiding the cup. In intinction the communicant retains the Host (with cupped hand over it lest it flutter away) until the chalice arrives, then, with one hand on the base of the chalice, he dips the edge of the Host in the cup and consumes it. In some parishes it is the custom for the administrator to take the Host and dip it into the cup and place it on the communicant's tongue. Crossing one's self and genuflecting are dictated by the practice of the parish and by one's inner feelings of appropriateness. So also is the response "Amen" after the words of administration have been said. (See BCP, pg. 834, Nos. 66 and 67, for appropriate prayers to use before and after receiving Communion.)

Ritual. The Book of Common Prayer, as the title page makes clear contains a variety of "rites and ceremonies." Ritual is the established or prescribed procedure for performing these rites and ceremonies. The ritual may have plain and simple dignity, or be very elaborate and ornate. But which ever way it is, it should be characterized by deep reverence. If the ritual truly expresses the devotion of the worshipers, it will be beautiful. An Irish priest once said, "It is not the color of the stole but the condition of the soul which matters most." A part of the genius of the Book of Common Prayer is that it provides for unity without requiring uniformity. For a particular congregation of worshipers the ritual to which they are accustomed through long practice has the validity of reverence and beauty which they bestow upon it.

That ritual, glorious to those who use it, might not appeal to worshipers in another tradition. It is the part of a loyal church person to recognize in others that liberty which is the common heritage of us all, and to conform as nearly as may be to the local custom. Truth has many aspects. Some of us see and appreciate and accent one part of it; some another. None of us comprehend the fullness of God's truth. The genius of the diversity which is seen in the worship of the Church from parish to parish reminds us that the truth is broader and higher and deeper than any single person or parish can comprehend and express.

PART TWO

After delving into what we see and experience in the Episcopal Church, the question comes to mind: What lies behind all these externals? To answer this we must look more deeply into their. . . .

. . . ESSENTIAL MEANING.

Chapter 12

The Church's Long Past: Early Beginnings

A good starting point for one who would seek the essential meaning that lies behind the services in which the Church engages is to look at the Church's history—where it came from. This will lead to a consideration of what it believes about itself and the world, and what it considers to be its reason for being. So let's look first at the Church's long past.

> The Church's one foundation
> Is Jesus Christ her Lord.

So wrote Samuel Stone, a clergyman-poet of the Church of England, in the 1860's in the opening words of what has become a beloved hymn. The truth of those words began to take shape when the risen Christ commissioned the apostles to be his witnesses to the very ends of the earth. The Old Testament had been the long story of God's chosen people Israel. Now, what came to be called "the new Israel" became its successor. The bestowal of the Holy Spirit and the commission to proclaim the Good News of God in Christ to all nations was the starting point (John 20:19-23 and Acts 2:1-11; Matthew 28:16-20 and Acts 1:8).

The Book of Acts is the history of that first generation after the Lord's crucifixion-resurrection and the Epistles contain literature of that period. The number of believers in the risen Lord grew rapidly. There were at first 120 (Acts 1:15). Not long after, thanks to Peter's fearless streetcorner preaching in Jerusalem, there were 3000 (Acts 2:14 and 41; see also 5:14). Then, because of persecution, the believers scattered throughout Judea, Samaria, and to Damascus and Caesarea (Acts 8:1; 9:2; 11:11-18), and, thanks chiefly to the missionary activity of Peter and Paul, of Barnabas and Mark, of Silas and others, the Church spread around the Mediterranean basin.

Naturally, as the Church began to increase in numbers and to spread, additional leadership had to be elected or appointed. This began to happen first in Jerusalem where the apostles needed assistance and appointed persons to serve under them (Acts 6:1-6). The Greek word for service is *diakonia* from which the title deacon is derived. It was not long before the practice developed of appointing elders to be in charge of each congregation (Acts 14:23; Titus 1:5). Elder is a venerable Old Testament title which was adopted by the Christian Church. The Greek word for elder is *presbuteros* which comes into English as presbyter and, eventually, another Old Testament title became its Christian equivalent, priest. There was a third development. When the apostles died the leadership·of the Church passed into the hands of overseers or guardians of groups of congregations (Acts 20:28; Titus 1:7). The Greek word for overseer is *episkopas* from which we get episcopal and episcopate, and, eventually, the title bishop. Bishops, then, are successors to the apostles in the leadership of the Church. So there came to be deacons, priests, and bishops in the young and growing Christian Church.

The reason Christians were persecuted (one of the factors which cause the Church to spread) was emperor-worship. The abler emperors of the Roman Empire had modified the ancient popular religions for patriotic reasons into worship of the State and its head. There was, of course, much more of patriotism than of religion in this system. The Christians, however, saw only the religious implications of the system and flatly refused to take part in emperor-worship. There is only one God and Father of all and he has revealed himself in Jesus Christ the Lord. There are no other gods; they would not violate the First Commandment. From the Roman point of view Christian refusal to worship the Emperor was treason.

The first extensive persecutions by the State were in Rome under Nero in 64 A.D., and similar persecutions continued sporadically and with varying degrees of intensity and cruelty until 323 when Emperor Constantine, who extolled freedom of conscience, finally became the sole ruler of the empire.

There were Christians everywhere in his far-flung empire, but they had differences among themselves. Constantine decided that if he could get the Christians to agree among themselves their ubiquitous presence could be the unifying factor of his realm. So he called a meeting at his summer palace at Nicea of Church leaders from all over the empire. That meeting was the Council of Nicea in 325, the first general council of the Church. From the Church's point of view that meeting was important for another reason.

In the centuries beyond New Testament times there

was serious division in the Church as to the true nature of Jesus Christ. The Christians believed he was entirely human "yet without sin" and at the same time "in him the fullness of God was pleased to dwell" (Hebrews 4:15 and Colossians 1:19). Others, who claimed to be Christians, contended that he was either a very noble man but not divine, or that he was a heavenly person and not really human. There were four great general councils of the Church with bishops and other representatives from all over Christendom which dealt with this issue. The familiar Nicene Creed came out of the first of these councils and it affirms that Jesus Christ who is "true God from true God" is also him who "came down from heaven . . . became incarnate of the Virgin Mary and was made man." The conclusion of the fourth general council, the Council of Chalcedon, 451, is also in the Prayer Book (BCP, 864). The points of view which vary from these statements are called heresies. While they were officially laid to rest in those early centuries they have continued to crop up time and again in various guises during the long life of the Church.

In the beginning, all bishops of the Church possessed equal authority. There were five great Christian centers —Jerusalem, Antioch, Alexandria, and Constantinople in the East, and Rome in the West. Each was independent and their bishops were usually called patriarchs. In time, the recognized authority these patriarchs possessed began to become less equal. Rome was the first city of the world—"the Eternal City," it was called—and, naturally, the influence of her bishop was very great. It is understandable, therefore, that the Bishop of Rome had a sense of supremacy. He considered himself the successor to St. Peter who had been martyred in Rome, the Vicar of Christ, and, before long, the head of the whole Church. Generally, his supremacy was recognized without question. The Eastern bishops, however, resisted the power of Rome. The Church of the East maintained its independence and has to this day. The story in England was different. Because that story of the Church of England is the link between the Episcopal Church in America today and the Christian Church of New Testament times, let's examine it.

Chapter 13

The Church's Long Past:
The Church of England

When, and exactly how, Christianity first reached the British Isles is unknown. The first evidence of its presence there is that British bishops attended the Council of Arles in France in 314, and were also among those who gave formal assent to the decisions of the Council of Nicea in 325.

In the course of the next 250 years Britain was invaded by Angles, Saxons, and Jutes from the European mainland. These peoples were heathens, Druids for the most part, and they pushed the native Britons back into the mountains of Scotland and Wales. Years later when Gregory, the Bishop of Rome, learned that the inhabitants of Britain were not Christians, he sent missionaries under the leadership of Augustine to convert them. As it happened, Ethelbert, the King of Kent and overlord of much of southeastern England had married a Christian princess named Bertha. Through her influence the missionaries were received kindly, and, in due course, the King was converted and was baptized on Christmas Day, 597. Augustine was ultimately named the first Archbishop of Canterbury. (The Archbishop of Canterbury who was installed in May, 1991 is the 103rd to hold that position.)

In the meantime, another development had taken

place in Ireland. In the course of a raid on the coast of Wales in 405, a young Christian named Patrick was seized and carried off to Ireland where he served as a slave for six years until he was able to escape to the continent. There he lived for years in the monastery of Lerins off the southern coast of France. In 432, he was ordained a missionary bishop and returned to northern Ireland where he established the Church which he served for the rest of his life. The Irish or Celtic Church which he founded also established a monastery on Iona, an island off the west coast of Scotland, and from there, in the seventh century, a missionary named Aidan began to evangelize the heathen inhabitants of northern and central England.

There were, therefore, two branches of Christendom in the British Isles in the seventh century—Roman Christianity, that, under the leadership of Augustine, had converted the peoples who had long before invaded the English midlands and lowlands, and Celtic Christianity, that probably had its genesis in the Eastern Church and which, under Aidan, had evangelized northern and central England. At the Council of Whitby in 664, these two branches of Christendom united to form what they called "The Church of England."

That Church, down through the centuries, was always more the Church *of* England than the Church *in* England. The English have always had a strong sense of national identity and have resisted foreign efforts to dominate them. Two signal indications of this spirit took place in the thirteenth century. The first was the Magna Carta, a political and constitutional document which the barons forced King John to sign in 1215. John was an ineffectual monarch both in the high-handed way in which he dealt with his subjects and in his involvement with foreign powers, including his relations with the Bishop of Rome. The Magna Carta stated in effect that "we, the people of England, are beholden to no one outside the realm," and further that "the Church of England is beholden to no one outside the realm."

The second indication of this independent spirit is seen in what happened in the relations of John Wycliffe, one of the towering religious leaders of that day, and the Bishop of Rome. Wycliffe was outspoken in his conviction that the Scripture is supreme in its authority and that the Church and the papacy had corrupted and overstepped the authority that was theirs. He attacked the spiritual tyranny of the ecclesiastical authority over people's lives by its claim that the priest alone could perform the miracle of Christ's presence in the Sacrament of the Altar, that the priest alone could grant or withhold the absolution that restored the sinner in the Sacrament of Penance. Wycliffe considered the power of the hierachy as a barrier to the free course of the Gospel. As well as being a fiery preacher, he was a considerable Biblical scholar and translated the Bible into English for the first time. The Pope denounced him and, no doubt, would have brought him to trial and condemned him to burn at the stake had he been able to get his hands on him. Wycliffe, however, lived out his days in the British Isles and never lowered his voice. This is another indication that the English would not tolerate religious dominance from outside the realm.

This brings us to the tumultuous days of the Reformation in the sixteenth century.

Chapter 14

The Church's Long Past:
The Reformation

The winds of change—political, social, and religious —were blowing strongly in Europe in the early years of the sixteenth century. It was the time when western Europe was beginning to break out of its feudal mold; when the modern world was being born. Society could no longer remain that of a noble, privileged class on top of a voiceless peasant-serf class that had no rights. There was an emerging middle class in the wings ready to come on stage. England had already seen gradual changes which turned the feudal serf into the independent yeoman-farmer some hundred years before. France, under a strong monarchy was to postpone the upheaval until the bloody, tumultuous days of the French Revolution. But in Germany the time was ripe; the clock had struck.

The occasion was the sale of papal indulgences, seen as the purchase of remittance of punishment in purgatory. The sale of indulgences, which poured gold into the papal coffers, was only symbolic of the corruptions which had been a part of Church practice during the Middle Ages. Martin Luther, an Augustinian monk and scholar, protested strongly the superstitious practices associated with the whole system of indulgences. Through the use of the new printing press, Luther's sweeping appeal from the authority of the pope to the authority of Scriptures spread rapidly through western Europe.

Once the sacramental system was attacked it was subjected to an increasing variety of interpretations. For
Luther, the reformed Mass, now a communion service
in the German vernacular, could retain all that was not
specifically forbidden by Scripture and remain sur-
rounded by much of its ancient beauty and traditional
ceremonies. To Zwingli, a Swiss protestant reformer,
the Lord's Supper was simply a memorial service. With
Calvin, the French protestant and father of Presbyteri-
anism, the emphasis shifted away from the Sacrament to
a sense of personal responsibility that nurtured a sturdy,
God-fearing moral character. The Anabaptists (or re-
baptizers) were a fanatical sect who lived by the Bible as
a book of law and insisted on the necessity of adult
baptism. All of these reforming pressures and others were
splintering the Church of western Europe away from the
Church of Rome.

The wind is not likely to blow strongly through the
trees on one bank of a stream without rustling the leaves
on the farther bank. Despite the vigilance of ecclesiastical
authorities, Lutheran books were smuggled into England
in large numbers and read widely by both clergy and lay
persons. Anabaptist and other influences followed in
the trail of Lutheranism. These fanned the embers of
resentment against the evils of the papal Church. The
Reformation in England, however, had a different character. The appeal had an important political twist: we
will resist papal authority partly because of papal corruptions, but, to no small degree, because we will not be
subjected to any foreign authority, temporal or spiritual.

Henry VIII, the religious, superstitious, powerful,
unscrupulous King of England, in his dealings with Pope

Clement VII over royal domestic affairs was only the catalyst that propelled Parliament into a series of historic decisions. That body, quoting from ancient documents reaffirmed that the sovereign State of England was rightly free from both "the annoyance of the see of Rome as well as from the authority of other foreign potentates." They made it clear that the Church *in* England was anciently and would continue to be the Church *of* England. The legislative assembly of the English Church (Convocation of the Clergy) declared solemnly that the Roman pontiff had no more authority in England than any other foreign bishop, and the orthodoxy of the National Church was proclaimed when Parliament assured the world that by none of its statutes was there any intention to "decline or vary from . . . the ancient Catholic faith of Christendom."*

The services of the Church continued but with a difference. The Bible had been translated into contemporary English during the years of the controversy with Rome and was beginning to be heard in the language of the people. After King Henry's death, Archbishop Cranmer was responsible for the publication in 1549 of the first Book of Common Prayer. The religion of the new Prayer Book was the religion of the Bible and this scriptural character accounts largely for the power of the Prayer Book in the minds and hearts of people through these intervening centuries. During the later reign of Elizabeth I, the Episcopal Church and its worship, essentially as we know it today, took shape.

*See P.M. Dawley, *Chapters in Church History* (The Church's Teaching: Volume Two), New York, The National Council, Protestant Episcopal Church, 1950, chapter 6, for a fuller account of this period of history.

Every watershed time in history like the Reformation has good and bad results, gains and losses. The effect on the quality of religious life both in the new and the re- formed churches and the Roman Church was of great benefit. New scholarship explored the deep meanings of the Christian faith. A new and deeper appreciation of the Lord's Supper came out of the controversy which raged over its meaning. And there was a wider involve- ment of people, lay as well as clerical, in the thinking, worship, governance, and mission of the Church. The negative effect of the Reformation was the fracturing of the Church into a number of independent Christian bodies—the Lutherans of Germany, the Calvinists or Presbyterians of Switzerland, the more extreme Puritans who are the ancestors of the New England Congregation- alists, the Baptists who are the descendants of the Anabaptists. And, through the years since, this tendency has continued. There are now more than 250 protestant denominations in the United States.

The Church of England has become, in succeeding centuries, the Mother Church of a considerable segment of Christendom. Along with the colonialization which created the far-flung British Empire there was the activity of missionary societies which established the Church of England around the world. Thus, there came into exist- ence the Anglican Communion, composed of those national Churches that recognize a certain spiritual primacy in the Archbishop of Canterbury. Today, there are some 18 of them, independent and self-governing, including the Church of England, the Church of Wales, the Church of Ireland, the Episcopal Church of Scotland, the Anglican Church of Canada, the Church of the

Province of the West Indies, the Churches of Australia, Burma, Japan, Africa, New Zealand, Brazil, (the Church of China may still exist) and the Episcopal Church in the United States.

Let's now turn to take a closer look at the Church in America.

Chapter 15

The Church's Long Past:
The Church in America

The Church of England first put down missionary roots in America in 1607 when an Anglican chaplain named Robert Hunt accompanied the London Company's band of explorer-settlers who landed at Jamestown Island in what came to be called Virginia. Chaplain Hunt was employed by the London Company to serve its people and he was accountable to the company. In later years, the parish minister in Virginia was accountable to his vestry rather than to any far-away bishop in England. In the northern colonies, the presence of the Church of England was part of the far-flung missionary work of the Society for the Propagation of the Gospel, and SPG clergy were responsible to the Society. There were no bishops in America and there was considerable opposition to having any. Bishops were members of the House of Lords and all British nobility were, by association, identified with the Crown and its alleged tyranny.

When the American Revolution came most Anglican clergy were Tories and identified themselves with the British cause. Some, however, were loyal to the colonies and served as chaplains in the Continental Line. During the war, churches were very short of ministers. After Independence, the almost leaderless Anglican Church struggled to find an identity separate from the Church of England, to develop an organization of its own, to determine what its Prayer Book should be like, even to find a new name. Within only a decade the Church had done all of these things.

The name "Protestant Episcopal Church" was first used in Maryland in 1780 as a description. *Episcopal,* of course, because the historic episcopacy was fundamental to its life. The age-old practices and beliefs of the Church—its sacraments, its creeds, its holy orders— were germane to its very being. But also *protestant,* a word that has become for some people little and negative compared to what it meant then. The Latin *protestatio* means "an open declaring of one's mind." In the Reformation it first concerned the political and religious freedom of the non-Roman Churches of Germany. This open declaring of one's mind involved protesting *against* the Church of Rome and against Roman authority. But that same open declaring meant to protest *for* religious freedom. To the Americans, it was freedom from English canon law which bound the Church of England to the British crown, as well as freedom from the authority of the Church of Rome. This description of the American Church as Catholic and yet free from both the British Crown and the Church of Rome became the official name of the Church in 1783: The Protestant Episcopal Church in the United States of America.

In spite of very great difficulties, Bishop Seabury of Connecticut was consecrated by three Scottish bishops in 1784. Three years later, Bishops White of Pennsylvania and Provoost of New York were consecrated by the Archbishop of Canterbury and two others, and not long after that, Bishop Madison of Virginia was consecrated also. At the first General Convention of the new Protestant Episcopal Church in 1789, delegates adopted a constitution and authorized their own Book of Common Prayer. "This Church is far from intending to depart from the Church of England in any essential point of doctrine, discipline, or worship," was stated pointedly in the Preface of that first American Prayer Book. The Protestant Episcopal Church in the United States of America is part of the Catholic Church of Christendom.

Its constitution set up a confederation of dioceses with a national structure somewhat similar to the United States Congress. There is a House of Bishops composed of all the bishops of the several dioceses and a House of Clerical and Lay Deputies. This latter body is composed of four clergy and four lay persons from each diocese. Official action by the National Church, such as the adoption of its Book of Common Prayer, has to pass both Houses of General Convention. The president of the House of Bishops is the Presiding Bishop, the representative head of the whole American Church. General Convention meets every three years and during the intervening time the Executive Council, composed of elected bishops, priests, and lay persons under the chairmanship of the Presiding Bishop conducts the business of the National Church. It is a representative system in which lay persons have a significant role.

It took a generation for this Church to gather its strength after the Revolution. Among the great leaders who ushered in the new day of vitality and mission were Bishop Hobart of New York, Bishop Griswold of the Eastern Diocese (New England), and Bishops Moore and Meade of Virginia. Tardily, in 1835, the Church began to take missionary responsibility seriously and began to spread through the west. The Methodists, the Baptists, and the Presbyterians were far ahead of them. During the next generation "foreign missions" were established in Texas, China, Japan, Liberia, and, before the end of the century, in the Philippine Islands, Alaska, Brazil, Central America, the West Indies, and the Hawaiian Islands. "The Church that lives to itself, dies to itself," said Michael Ramsey, Archbishop of Canterbury, in 1963. The Episcopal Church was not going to suffer that fate.

Two movements that started in England had a profound influence on the American Church. Back about the time George Washington was born, an English clergyman named John Wesley caught a vision of a renewed and revitalized Church in a day when the Church of England was in a sad and decadent state. He and other young men at Oxford formed what was shortly nicknamed "The Holy Club" to deepen their own spiritual lives. The rule or spiritual method (hence *Methodist*) they followed eventuated in a tireless concern to evangelize. Methodist curcuit riders began reaching significant numbers of people in America in the latter part of the eighteenth century. Their influence on the Anglican Church both in England and in America was seen in the number of evangelical priests who stressed personal piety, evangelical outreach, and the saving power of the Cross. They turned their backs on the self-concern of the Church with the minutiae of ritual and ceremony. They were not interested in the Church's catholic past or its sacramental significance. Such was the Evangelical Movement.

Just as the Evangelical Movement was the significant influence on the life of the Church in the eighteenth century, so was the Catholic Revival in the nineteenth century. Again, it started with a group of Oxford scholars. In the 1830's, they began the publication of a series of tracts that sought to make it clear that the Church of England could provide answers within the framework of a long-ignored heritage of catholic theology. The Church was absolute in its claims upon people, standing over against the world in proclaiming man's salvation through his membership in that divine society. Hence, the concern of the tractarians was with the authority with which the Savior has endowed his Church and with the essential sacramental character of its corporate life. This Oxford Movement, as it came to be called, had a profound influence on the life of the Church on both sides of the Atlantic.

Both the Evangelical Movement and the Catholic Revival recalled Anglicans to forgotten aspects of their heritage and tradition, and over the years they both have enriched the life of Anglicanism. This did not come about without a bitter struggle in the course of which false opposition labels—"High Church" and "Low Church"—came into being. Also, unfortunately, the terms *Catholic* and *Evangelical* with their great Christian significance were degraded into merely narrow partisan tags.

In the twentieth century, the Churches of Christendom began to move slowly toward one another. In 1927 the Episcopal Church took part in the first World Faith and Order Conference at Lausanne, Switzerland, where there were representatives of all the leading Christian bodies except for the Roman Catholic Church. A generation later, the Consultation on Church Union brought representatives of half a dozen Christian Churches including the Episcopal Church around the conference table to discuss what they had in common. Some 17 other Christian Churches, including the Roman Catholic, had official observers present. Pope Paul VI of Rome and Athenagoras I, Orthodox Patriarch of Constantinople, met and embraced on December 7, 1965. This was the first meeting since their predecessors had each excommunicated the offending other Church back in 1054. Several Archbishops of Canterbury, including the present Archbishop, and several Presiding Bishops of the Episcopal Church have sat down with the Bishop of Rome to discuss their differences. The Episcopal Church has commissions which are in friendly conversations with the Lutherans, the Roman Catholics, the Pentecostals, and others.

Are the winds of change blowing strongly over the divided Churches of Christendom? What will our Lord have the Church of tomorrow to be like?

Chapter 16

The Characteristics of the Church

In looking over the long life of the Episcopal Church we discover several distinctive characteristics that, during the last 400 odd years, seem to stand out.

**There is a concern that the Church of the present maintain its connection with the life and practice of the Church during its long past. At the time of the Reformation, the Church of England had no intention of breaking with the Church that had come down from ancient times through the Middle Ages. At the time of the Revolution, the Church in America maintained its continuity with the Church of England. The ancient offices of bishops, priests, and deacons were treasured and maintained.

**The authority of Scripture is always paramount, and the services of the Book of Common Prayer are grounded in it.

**Worship is in the language of the people.

**The laity have a significant and necessary role in the Church's worship.

This Church shares also in those characteristics that are the hallmark of the age-old Christian Church. In the Nicene Creed we proclaim that "we believe in one holy catholic and apostolic Church." What do these words mean? The Church is *one* because, in spite of its many divisions, it has one Head—Jesus Christ is its one Lord. The Church is *holy* because the Holy Spirit dwells in it, consecrates its members, and guides them in fulfilling God's mission to the world. The New Testament calls church members "saints" which means, literally, "the holy ones" (1 Corinthians 1:2). One American theologian has called the Holy Spirit the *esprit de corps* of the Church. So the analogy of school spirit can help us appreciate something of what this means. The Church is *catholic* because it is commissioned to teach *all* the revelation of God to *all* classes and conditions of people in *all* the world and every age. When we pray for "thy holy Church universal" (BCP, pg. 815) we are praying for the Catholic Church in all of its inclusiveness. Finally, the Church is *apostolic* because its faith, its sacraments, and its ministry have all come down from the apostles. The Church, through the centuries, has devoted itself "to the apostles' teaching and fellowship, to the breaking of bread, and the prayers" (Acts 2:42).

Practically and historically, we speak of the "Catholic Church" as that organized form of Christianity that was founded by Christ and his apostles and has maintained a continuous unbroken existence from the time of the apostles to the present. The Episcopal Church in the United States of America is a part of that Church of the ages. The *Te Deum* refers to the Catholic Church as "The holy Church throughout all the world," and in the Eucharist our conception of its breadth and extent takes a giant step when we join our praises "with Angels and Archangels, and with all the company of heaven." The holy Church universal is truly "a wonderful and sacred mystery."

In 1886, the House of Bishops wrestled with the question: What are the essential characteristics of the

Church? The bishops were making friendly gestures toward other branches of Christendom, and said that these are the "principles we believe to be the substantial deposit of Christian Faith and Order committed by Christ and his Apostles to the Church . . . and therefore incapable of compromise or surrender." At the Lambeth Conference two years later (that conference is the meeting of all the bishops of the Anglican Communion once every decade) the same four principles were endorsed. Here then are those principles that the Episcopal Church considers basic to its very existence:

1. The Holy Scriptures of the Old and New Testaments, as "containing all things necessary to salvation," and as being the rule and ultimate standard of faith.

2. The Apostles' Creed, as the Baptismal Symbol; and the Nicene Creed, as the sufficient statement of the Christian faith.

3. The two Sacraments ordained by Christ Himself— Baptism and the Supper of the Lord—ministered with unfailing use of Christ's words of Institution, and of the elements ordained by Him.

4. The Historic Episcopate, locally adapted in the methods of its administration to the varying needs of the nations and peoples called to God into the Unity of His Church (BCP, pg. 877-878).

If these four principles, known as "The Lambeth Quadrilateral," are the basic stuff of the Episcopal Church, then we should take a careful look at them for they are also basic to an understanding of this Church. So now we turn to a consideration of Holy Scriptures, the Creeds, the Sacraments, and the ordained ministry.

Chapter 17

Holy Scriptures

The Holy Scriptures, commonly called the Bible, are composed of the 39 books of the Old Testament and 27 books of the New Testament. There are 15 additional books in what is called the Apocrypha. They are not considered canonical, however, and are often not included. The Bible contains God's plan of salvation for us human beings, or as the Prayer Book puts it, "contains all things necessary to salvation."

The word *bible* means books. Holy Scriptures is a library of books, written by many different authors, in different periods of history. There is a variety of kinds of literature—history, poetry, prophecy, law, fiction, letters, reminiscences.* From all of it, the reader gets the unfolding story of how faith in God was gradually revealed . . . How people could come to confess, "I believe in God, the Father almighty, maker of heaven and earth." . . . And later, "And in Jesus Christ his only Son our Lord." . . . And finally, "I believe in the Holy Spirit" and "the holy catholic Church." This sacred library of books records God's dealings with the human race from the beginning of the world through the

---

*For a listing of the books according to category see: Robt. A. Bennett and O.C. Edwards, *The Bible for Today's Church* —*The Church Teaching Series* (New York: The Seabury Press, 1979), p. 16-18.

opening century of the Christian era.

Also, the Bible gives us insights about humankind. In the way in which people responded to and reacted in the face of God's initiative we see a reflection of ourselves. The Bible tells us as much about humankind and what we are like as it does about God and what he is like.

The profound and wonderful thing about the Bible is that it is the inspired Word of God. By this we mean that God has caused the Bible to be written in such a way that we experience his presence and power from reading it or hearing it read. For example, when we read "The Lord is my shepherd; I shall not want" (Psalm 23:1), we do not think of it as a bit of poetry written in probably 1000 B.C. Rather, it speaks directly to us in the present: "The Lord is *my* shepherd; *I* shall not want." So the Bible, like no other book, has an eternal quality which we describe as the inspired Word of God.

The Bible is the Church's book. It was the leaders of the Church under the guidance of the Holy Spirit who determined which books were to be contained in Holy Scriptures. The Church, therefore, under the guidance of the Holy Spirit is the true interpreter of what the Bible teaches. We, of course, can learn many things from it on our own, but, in the final analysis, the Church is its true interpreter.

Every church member is involved in both public and private reading of the Bible. On Sundays, Holy Scripture is read to us in church in the pattern of proclaiming and teaching the drama of redemption. The scheduled readings follow the Church Year (see Chapter 19). These readings are in a three-year cycle—Year A is built around Matthew's Gospel, Year B around Mark's Gospel, and

Year C around Luke's Gospel (BCP, pg. 888ff).

A person's daily private devotions may follow the "Daily Office Lectionary" (BCP, pg. 934ff). However, many find it more rewarding to follow a daily devotional guide like *Forward Day-by-Day* which is available on the tract rack of most parish churches. That booklet contains a passage of Scripture and a brief explanation for each day that relates it to everyday living. Many people follow those daily readings regularly. One of those was Duke Ellington who wrote:

> Ever since I saw the first copy, this little book has been my daily reading. It is clear, easy to understand, written in the language of the ordinary man, and always says things I want to know. (*Music is My Mistress,* p. 282)

When you feel ready to try reading the Bible book by book, *don't* try to read through the books in sequence starting with Genesis. Remember, the Bible is a library of books. No one would use a public library in that way —reading book after book across the shelves regardless of the subject matter. The best place to begin is with the life of Jesus in Mark. Then, perhaps, one of the other gospels, for each gives a slightly different view of him and some special details. After the Gospels take a look at the history of the early Church in Acts. A few letters of Paul will give you a feel for some of the thinking of the early Christians. Now, you may want to dip into a bit of the Old Testament history. Turn to Exodus, Joshua, Judges, 1 and 2 Samuel, and 1 and 2 Kings. After that perhaps a few of the prophets—Amos, Hosea, Isaiah, Jeremiah. If you like poetry, the Book of Psalms and Isaiah 40-66 can be very rewarding.

Devotional Bible reading is a next step. It is not Bible study such as a Bible class might do. It is rather seeking to become involved personally with the Word of God, and to make some sort of response to that Word and God's mighty acts. One helpful procedure is to accent all the pronouns that are in the first person. Take Psalm 130, for example:

> Out of the depths have *I* called to you, O Lord;
> Lord, hear *my* voice;
> Let your ears consider well the voice of *my* supplication.

Another helpful procedure is to read the letters of Paul as though you were a member of the congregation to which they were addressed.

It is a short step from reading the Bible in such a way as to make it one's own, and meditation. The latter is a spiritual exercise in response to the passage at hand, especially the story of the life of Jesus. Bishop Coburn suggests this procedure:

1. To picture a Biblical scene,
2. To ponder its meaning,
3. To promise God something as a result.

One technique is to imagine yourself one of the characters in the story—how would you feel, what would you say or do? Then, what do you think God is saying to you through this story? Finally, commit yourself to some concrete action, no matter how small, to implement what you have gained from the meditation. (These suggestions and others are found in *The Bible for Today's Church* mentioned above and in the books it lists for further reading.)

A fascinating way to get into the Bible's story and its

meaning is to read two books by Alan T. Dale—*Winding Quest—The Heart of the Old Testament in Plain English* and *New World—The Heart of the New Testament in Plain English* (Wilton, CT: Morehouse-Barlow Co., 1973). I can't recommend these books too highly for those who want to learn what the Bible is all about and how to appreciate it.

Chapter 18

The Faith of the Church—The Creeds

What the Christian believes is summed up in the Apostles' and Nicene Creeds. This is the faith of the Church, the revelation God gave through Jesus Christ, and what we believe about the Church is an integral part of this good news of God in Christ.

First, let's get a clear picture of what the creeds are.

The Apostles' Creed is called that because its roots go back literally to the time of the apostles. It attained its present wording gradually as the creed declared by candidates for baptism or by their sponsors in answer to direct questions. That ancient interrogatory form of this creed is found in the service of Holy Baptism (BCP, pg. 304).

The Nicene Creed was drawn up, as we saw earlier, by the first great General Council of the Church meeting at Nicea in the year 325. It is a fuller statement of the truths contained in the Apostles' Creed, especial emphasis being laid on the divinity of our Lord and on the work of the Holy Spirit. This is the creed which is used in the Eucharist. Because it is the credal statement drawn up by a body of people, its original form was in the plural: "*We* believe in one God . . ." (BCP, pg. 326).

There is a third credal statement which is known as "The Creed of Saint Athanasius." Athanasius was Bishop of Alexandria, Egypt, in the fourth century and was a strong and competent defender of the faith. This credal statement is identified with him although it is probably of much later origin. The Athanasian Creed is used on occasion in the Church of England. It has no official standing in our Church except as a historical document (BCP, pg. 864).

The Apostles' and Nicene Creeds have the authority of the whole Church behind them. They have also the complete individual accent of every member of the Church who believes what he is saying when he uses the words, "I believe *in* God. . . ." "In" is the biggest little word with which we describe a personal relationship. If the creed were an argument it would state, "I believe *that* there is a God who. . . ." Such a statement could be quite logical, but it would be impersonal and would not involve us. But when I say, "I believe *in* . . .," everything is different. Suppose I was talking about my next door neighbor. I could say "I believe that I have a neighbor named Carl Smith," and not know him very well or even be on speaking terms. But when I say, "I believe *in* my neighbor, Carl Smith," personal relations and commitment are involved immediately. I would endorse his check. He would lend me his hedgeclippers. We are trusting friends. So it is with the creed. "I believe in God" means that I am personally involved with him. He cares about me and sent his Son—"for us and for our salvation he came down from heaven . . . and was made man." I love him. I trust him. I want to serve him faithfully. When we say "I believe" or join in saying "We believe," we are really saying, "I bet my life on this relationship."

If a two-month-old baby could talk and reason

logically, here is what he might say in answer to the question "Why do you believe your mother loves you?" "I believe she loves me because she holds me close and cuddles me, she comforts me, she feeds me with her very self, she rocks me and sings to me, she tucks me in and watches over me." Verbs, verbs, verbs, verbs. That is what a deep and lasting personal relationship is made up of. Now look at the creeds. Jesus Christ was conceived, born, suffered, crucified, died, buried, descended, rose, ascended, is seated, will come again . . . Verbs describing all that God has done for you and me. Dr. Theodore Wedel used to say, "The Creed is a love story." And then he would go on to explain that the Almighty Father who made us and loved us so much that he gave us the freedom to grow as persons saw that we had gotten off the track and strayed like lost sheep. So he sent his Son to redeem us (*redeem* means "to make good again"). He lived and died and rose again that we might have life in all of its fullness. However, when he ascended, he did not leave us to flounder like helpless orphans and fall back into sin, he gave us his victorious Spirit and banded us together in a company embued by that Spirit, called the Church, that we might live in his presence now and forever.

While we worship only one God, the creeds each have three paragraphs—about God the Father, God the Son, and God the Holy Spirit. The Christian believes in one God who is at the same time three-in-one, the Holy Trinity. How can this be? The Trinity is difficult to understand no matter what one's age or education. Perhaps an analogy will help. Take the story of a book. It first exists in the mind of the author. No one can see it, but it is very real even though the author has not yet put it down on paper. Then he writes the book and it is published. It becomes something everyone can see, handle, examine, read. The day of publication is its birthday. Then one day it ceases to be published and circulated; it goes out of print. But it continues to have an influence. It is quoted and appears in footnotes long after it ceases to be available. This is the story of one book, but it has had three manifestations, each different, each real. In a way this helps us appreciate the mystery of the Holy Trinity. The triune God depicted in the creeds has three manifestations. He is God the Father, Creator of heaven and earth—unseen but very real. He is God the Son, Jesus Christ our Lord—he came into history at a definite time, he lived, suffered, died, and he is remembered to have said, "He who has seen me has seen the Father" (John 14:9). He is God the Holy Spirit—the Spirit that inspires the Church and her members is like the Jesus of Nazareth whom the disciples once knew. The Spirit, said Jesus, "will glorify me, for he will take what is mine and declare it to you" (John 16:14).

Chapter 19

The Faith of the Church—The Church Year

The Bible is the story of God's great acts of redemption. In the practice of the Church its story is told in two other ways. It is compressed into the creeds—our affirmations of faith. And it is stretched out and tacked down on the year's calendar so that we may celebrate every phase of its unfolding wonderfulness every year. Here is that story of redemption in its three forms:

Bible	Creeds	Seasons of the Church Year
Old Testament	First paragraph: "I believe in God the Father. . . ."	Advent
Matthew Mark Luke John	Second paragraph: I believe in Jesus Christ, his only Son our Lord. . . ."	Christmas Epiphany Lent Easter Ascension
Book of Acts The Epistles Book of Revelation	Third paragraph: "I believe in the Holy Spirit. . . ."	Pentecost

There are seven seasons of the Church Year. *Advent* tells us of the preparation for the coming of our Lord as the Babe of Bethlehem, and bids us prepare for his second coming to judge the world. It is also a preparation

90

for the annual Christmas festival. *Advent* means *coming*.

Christmas commemorates the nativity of our Lord—the coming of God's Son into the world. This wonderful mystery is called the incarnation. (*Incarnation* means coming "in the flesh.") The Creed describes it in these words, "by the power of the Holy Spirit he became incarnate from the Virgin Mary and was made man."

Epiphany commemorates the fact that Jesus is the Savior of the whole world. The Magi who came to worship him represent all the gentiles (nations) of the world. He is truly "a light to enlighten the nations and the glory of my people Israel." So Epiphany is a missionary season, a time of outreach. The word *epiphany* means *to make manifest* or *to shine forth*.

Lent is a forty-day season of preparation for Easter. It begins with our remembrance of the Lord's forty days of spiritual preparation in the wilderness after his baptism and before he began his ministry. So it is a time of spiritual discipline and of self-denial. The last week of Lent is called Holy Week. It commemorates the events of the last week of Jesus' earthly life—the triumphal entry into Jerusalem on Palm Sunday, the Last Supper on Maundy Thursday, and the crucifixion on Good Friday.

Easter commemorates our Lord's resurrection from the dead. This earliest of Christian celebrations covers forty days and ends with the risen Lord's ascension into heaven. Easter is so important as the cornerstone of the Christian faith that it is not only celebrated annually, it is also celebrated weekly. Every Sunday is a little Easter —"the weekly remembrance of the glorious resurrection of thy Son our Lord" (BCP, pg. 56).

Ascension tells of the risen Lord's triumphant return to heaven.

Pentecost commemorates the coming of the Holy Spirit. This Spirit of God who once spoke through the prophets, then was embodied in Jesus, now becomes the Spirit of the Church—the inspiration and guide of its members individually and collectively. (See page 25 for the liturgical colors associated with the days and seasons of the Church Year.)

A number of details about the observance of the various seasons and days of the Church Year are set forth in the Prayer Book, pages 15-18. There also is a listing of the principal feasts and other holy days of the Church Year. In addition the Prayer Book contains a calendar of saints' days (pages 19-30) which may be observed through the year. The propers for these days as well as a biographical sketch of each person are to be found in *Lesser Feasts and Fasts* (New York: The Seabury Press, 1980).

Chapter 20

The Sacraments

The workings of a person's mind and spirit are only a part of the process by which the meaning of the Good News of the Christian faith comes into a human life. The sacraments provide another and deeper level of involvement. They are outward and visible signs of inward and spiritual grace which Christ has given us. The outward signs, the basic actions of sacraments, are washing, eating, and drinking. Those basic desires for sustaining and intensifying the forces of life that all of us have are used as the vehicles through which God's grace is given us. The Prayer Book defines grace as "God's favor towards us, unearned and undeserved." By it "God forgives our sins, enlightens our minds, stirs our hearts, and strengthens our wills." And the sacraments have been given us by our Lord in the Gospels as the "sure and certain means by which we receive that grace" (BCP, pgs. 857-58).

There is more to being a Christian than a personal faith in the redeeming act of God in Christ. One must be a part of the community in which the effects of Christ's redeeming work of reconciliation and love become actual and are nurtured. The sacraments are the instruments whereby the individual is made a member of God's covenant community and is subjected to its disciplines and responsibilities. In the sacraments both the personal and social relationships of Christian salvation are publicly ratified, accepted, and communicated.

Holy Baptism. Holy Baptism is the sacrament through which a person is born into God's family, the Christian Church. The sacrament is a solemn agreement or covenant which the candidate (or his godparents on his behalf) makes with God. God's part of the agreement is that the person's sins are forgiven and he enters upon a new life of grace as a member of the household of God. For his part, the candidate accepts Jesus Christ as his Savior and promises to follow him as his Lord. Then, after stating his belief in God—Father, Son, and Holy Spirit —in the words of the Apostles' Creed, he promises that with God's help his new life of grace will follow this pattern:

1) he will continue in the apostles' teachings and fellowship, in the breaking of bread, and in the prayers;

2) he will persevere in resisting evil, and, whenever he falls into sin, repent and return to the Lord;

3) he will proclaim by word and example the Good News of God in Christ;

4) he will seek and serve Christ in all persons, loving his neighbor as himself; and

5) he will strive for justice and peace among all people, and respect the dignity of every human being.

This is a big order, but it is what it means to be a member of God's Family, the Church.

Because we recognize that the candidate cannot do all this without the help of God's grace and the support of the other members of his heavenly family, we first thank the Heavenly Father that in this sacrament he has raised this person "to the new life of grace" and we pray that the Lord will sustain him with his Holy Spirit. Then we, his fellow forgiven sinners for whom Christ died, receive him "into the household of God" (BCP, pg. 308).

The water of baptism (the outward and visible sign of this sacrament) and the sign of the cross on his forehead are the stamps of approval on this solemn agreement between the Heavenly Father and the newly-received member of the household of God.

Baptisms are usually administered by ordained clergy —the priest or bishop usually, but it may be administered by a deacon. In cases of emergency, however, any baptized person may administer this sacrament. In such a case it should be reported to the rector of the parish and properly recorded in the Parish Register (BCP, pgs. 313-14).

In early times when adults were baptized their children were baptized along with them and brought up in the Christian faith (Acts 16:33). So the practice of baptizing infants is a venerable one. We are never too young to become members of God's Family, and to receive the gift of God's grace. Parents and godparents or sponsors take the baptismal vows on behalf of the little ones. Then, when the children are old enough to speak for themselves, they renew those vows themselves at Confirmation which we shall examine later.

The Holy Eucharist. We have already examined the Holy Eucharist as the principal Sunday service (Chapter 8). We now look at it again as a sacrament given by Christ as the means whereby we receive God's strengthening grace. In considering Baptism, we learned that those who are baptized and have become members of God's Family, the Church, have committed themselves to a way of life that is beyond their ability to accomplish apart from the help of God's grace and the support of the other members of the Body of Christ. That much-needed continual spiritual strengthening has been provided for us by our Lord in this sacrament of his Body and Blood.

The two characteristics of this sacrament—the outward and visible, the inward and spiritual—have been clearly recognized from the beginning. Jesus on the night before his death took a most ordinary and easily-understood practice of daily life—a common meal—and transformed it into a holy meal, the vehicle of God's strengthening grace. Just as physical food strengthens our bodies, so the grace of our Lord Jesus Christ strengthens our souls in this sacrament. (Reread the section "Bread and Wine" in the chapter on the Symbolism of Worship, page 23).

The risen Christ comes to us in this sacrament. He is present when his faithful ones gather at his Table. Although we don't know exactly how our Lord is present under the forms of bread and wine, we believe that he is truly present. It is a real presence and not merely an imaginary one. Much has been written to try to explain it, but it is still a holy mystery as we say in the service (BCP, pg. 339).

Whether our preparation to receive the sacrament is made confidentially in the presence of a priest or is our private spiritual exercise depends on the practice of us as individuals and of our parish. However, it should always follow a similar pattern—repentance and confession, reconciliation and resolve, and faith that we will receive God's strengthening grace when we come to the Lord's Table.

A helpful pattern of preparation for receiving the sacrament is set forth in the Invitation to commune (BCP, pg. 330). Fill in details of what each part of that Invitation means to you on this particular occasion as you look forward to receiving the gift of grace. Here is a way to do it:

1) *Ye who do truly and earnestly repent you of your sins.* Exactly what is it that I think or do that keeps me from being the kind of person I know our Lord wants me to be? Be specific.

2) *And are in love and charity with your neighbors.* Have I actually tried to make up with the person or persons from whom I have become estranged? With God's help I can do it.

3) *And intend to lead a new life following the commandments of God and walking from henceforth in his holy ways.* What new pattern of behavior do I intend to follow with the help of the strengthening grace I expect to receive shortly at the Lord's Table? Exactly what do I intend to do?

4) *Draw near with faith.* I firmly expect that the gracious Lord will, in this Holy Meal, give me the necessary strength to live up to the resolve I have just made.

Fasting is, for a number of people, a part of their preparation for coming to the Supper of the Lord. Some fast overnight, others for several hours before the service. It is an ancient custom, but is not required by the Church and it is certainly not expected of the sick or elderly. In any case the decision is one's own, a personal and private discipline.

The Five Sacramental Rites. When we get beyond the two Gospel sacraments that were instituted by our Lord, we run into honest disagreement among conscientious Church people. How many other sacraments are there? How do we consider Confirmation, Ordination, Holy Matrimony, Reconciliation of a Penitent, and Unction? These are certainly special rites through which God's grace comes to his faithful people on significant occasions. They are surely more than mere sacred signs, yet they are not sacraments of the same rank with the Gospel sacraments of Baptism and the Lord's Supper. The Prayer Book recognizes this difference by calling them "Sacramental Rites." They each have a pastoral dimension because each is used at a spiritual milestone moment in a person's life as we have discussed earlier in dealing with the Pastoral Offices of the Prayer Book (Chapter 10).

For a description of the meaning and significance of each of the five Sacramental Rites turn to:

page 110, Confirmation,

page 99, Ordination,

page 48, Holy Matrimony,

page 49, Reconciliation of a Penitent, and

page 49, Unction (see Ministration to the Sick).

Chapter 21

The Ordained Ministry

The risen Lord said to the apostles, "As the Father has sent me, even so send I you" (John 20:21). (*Apostle* means "one who is sent out.") So they went forth in his Name to proclaim the Good News of God in Christ to the ends of the earth. Because of time and circumstance, the Church's leadership in carrying out the Lord's Great Commission became the responsibility of bishops, priests or presbyters, and deacons. We saw how these orders of the ordained ministry evolved in the story of the early years of the Church following the crucifixion-resurrection (Chapter 12).

Down through the centuries, the solemn rite of making or ordaining each new generation of clergy has continued unbroken. With the laying on of hands and prayer, the candidate receives the authority and power to be a deacon, a priest, or a bishop in the Church of God. The bishop alone may ordain a deacon, laying hands on his head. The bishop and attending presbyters or priests lay hands on the head of one being ordained priest, and three bishops must take part and lay hands on one being ordained bishop. (These services are found in the "Episcopal Services" section of the Prayer Book, page 509ff.) Bishops are not only central to the making and transmitting of this ordained authority in the life of the Church, they are also the visible link between the Church of the present and the apostles. The creed describes the Church as "catholic" and "apostolic" and bishops are symbolic of an aspect of what these words try to convey. Catholic: they remind us of the universality of the Church back through the ages. Apostolic: they are successors to the apostles and our link with the Church of their day. This is why the Historic Episcopacy (sometimes called "Apostolic Succession") is important and is a part of the Lambeth Quadrilateral (Chapter 16).

The following are the duties and responsibilities of the ordained ministers of the Church:

A bishop is the chief priest and pastor of a diocese, and all other clergy derive their ministry from him or her. He or she is the guardian of the faith, responsible to see that the full truth of the Gospel of God in Christ is proclaimed. He administers the discipline of the Church and is responsible to see that the official worship of the Church is regularly used in the churches under his care. It is as this representative person that the bishop presides at a baptism, when present, for the individual being baptized is becoming a member of the one, holy, catholic, and apostolic Church in its broadest sense. It is also in this capacity that he administers Confirmation and ordains persons to the ministry. There are several kinds of assistant bishops. A *bishop coadjutor* is one who has been elected by the diocese and consecrated to assist in the work of the diocese and will ultimately succeed to the bishopric. A *suffragan bishop* is one who assists the diocesan bishop, but has no right of succession. A bishop who is an *assistant-to-the-bishop* is one who was not elected by the diocese but is a bishop who has been employed by the diocesan bishop to assist him.

A priest (presbyter is another New Testament name for this office) is the regular minister of a parish. He or she is the spiritual leader of the members of the congregation. At ordination, a priest receives authority to proclaim the Gospel, administer the sacraments, bless and pardon in God's Name. It is his responsibility to be a faithful pastor, a patient teacher, and a wise councilor to those committed to his care. When in full charge he or she is called the *rector*, and his assistants, whether priest or deacons, are usually called *curates*. A *vicar* is a priest in charge of a chapel to a parish church, or a mission of the diocese where he represents the bishop, the chief missionary. A *dean* is the priest in charge of a cathedral church. A priest who has general oversight of the missions of a diocese under the bishop (or some other well-defined diocesan responsibility) is sometimes known as an *archdeacon*.

A *deacon* is an ordained assistant to the bishop or to the rector of a parish. He or she may assist in the administration of the sacraments and may preach. His or her chief role is to assist and to serve those in need. Usually a deacon is advanced to the priesthood after serving one year. A perpetual deacon is one, often engaged in secular work, who is ordained to assist in a parish or elsewhere without being advanced to the priesthood.

Religious or monastic orders are another kind of full time ministry in the Church. These are groups of men or women who live together in a community and dedicate themselves, soul and body, to the service of God, renouncing all other personal ties and relationships. They are under lifelong vows of chastity (they do not marry), poverty (they may not own property), and obedience.

Each order has its own distinctive garb or habit. The house of an order of men is called a monastery; the one for an order of women is called a convent. There are a number of monastic orders in the Episcopal Church.

Chapter 22

The Mission of the Church

When we considered the long life of the Church, we noted its phenomenal growth—from 120, to 3000, to large numbers of people throughout the whole Roman Empire (the whole of the then-known world) by 325. The disciples remembered the risen Lord's words: "Go and make disciples of all nations" and ". . . you shall receive power when the Holy Spirit has come upon you; and you shall be my witnesses . . . to the end of the earth" (Matthew 28:19; Acts 1:8). The Good News of God in Christ is that the Heavenly Father loves human-kind so much that he sent his Son to show us how to have life in all of its abundance and who died for our sins that we might have eternal life. This is the Gospel that, in the course of the centuries, was proclaimed to nations and people around the globe.

In the second half of the twentieth century, there have been new developments in the missionary outreach of the Church. Earlier Christian missionaries were sent out to "take Christ to the heathen." The Christian missions which were established were, in a sense, colonies of the Church back home. Gradually, the point of view changed. Christ is not the possession of the Christian "Haves" to be shared with the non-Christian "Have-nots." He is already there. Perhaps he is not fully known, appreciated, worshiped, but he is there nonetheless.

Christian missionaries share what Christ means to them and are open to receive as well as to give. They are concerned to train native leaders so that the Church may be strong and self-governing. In the 1960's the key phrase was "mutual responsibility and interdependence in the Body of Christ."

The practice is spreading of dioceses establishing partnerships with dioceses in distant places. A diocese in the United States enters into a partnership with one in another part of the world. They work out a mutual help and support program. They study each other's needs and work to supply them. This involves each in praying for the other, in sending visiting missionaries to the other, and in supplying those special needs of which one diocese is rich and the other poor. These needs are various. For example, a fast-growing African diocese may send someone to its American partner diocese to conduct a teaching and evangelizing series of missions. In its turn, the American diocese may send an agricultural expert and equipment to that African partner diocese. Sometimes the help is financial, and, always, each prays regularly for that branch of the Church in the other diocese. So it goes: partners miles apart helping each other carry out the Great Commission.

Another kind of missionary outreach is developing also—it might be called intensive rather than extensive. In our industrial society, there are large numbers of people whose lives are blighted by conditions over which they have no control. The few acres of a small farmer are gobbled up by a large mechanized farming operation when the little farmer cannot survive bad times. He moves to the city hoping to find work. The cheap, poorer housing of the city becomes overcrowded and there are not enough jobs to go around. Or the plant in a one-industry town is closed down by a board of directors miles away and a whole community becomes destitute. As Canon Lloyd Casson told the Executive Council in February, 1980, "The Gospel is not believable unless the churches relate to the neighborhoods of which they are a part."* Thus, the Church has another kind of commission from her Lord: responsibility to feed the hungry, clothe the naked, heal the sick, be the harbinger of comfort and caring and hope (Luke 4:16-21; Matthew 25:31-46). The bishops of those dioceses in which there are cities blighted by ghettoes and slums are spear-heading the Church's deep concern to bring the Good News of life in all of its fullness to the people whose lives are devastated by circumstances they cannot change. This might be called the new missionary frontier.

How we can share in the mission of the Church at home and overseas is our next consideration. The Lord's injunction to go into all the world in his Name is addressed to every baptized Christian.

---

*Casson was president of the Episcopal Urban Coalition. Quoted in *The Living Church,* July 6, 1980, page 6.

PART THREE

This look at the Episcopal Church has convinced me that the holy catholic Church is the Heavenly Father's agent for helping people live their God-intended lives at their best, both here and beyond the grave. Because I want to share in proclaiming that Good News that came into the world through Jesus Christ, I want to know how I can be a responsible member of the Church and how I make that . . .

. . . COMMITMENT.

Chapter 23

The Ministry of the Laity

When we discussed the ministry a few pages back (Chapter 21), we carefully spoke only of the ordained ministry. At that point, we intentionally passed over the most numerous, most significant category of Christian ministers: lay persons. The Prayer Book outlines their ministry in this way:

> The ministry of lay persons is to represent Christ and his Church; to bear witness to him wherever they may be; and, according to the gifts given them, carry on Christ's work of reconciliation in the world; and to take their place in the life, worship, and governance of the Church (BCP, pg. 855).

Every baptized person's occupation in shop or field, in office or school or home is his "church work." That is the place where he or she carries on a witness to the saving power of God in Christ; Paul called it a "ministry of reconciliation" (II Corinthians 5:18). In addition, many lay persons assist in the worship and governance of the Church. They carry on this second kind of church work as layreaders, choir members, acolytes, ushers, Sunday school teachers, vestrypersons, and in a host of other significant roles that make the Church's worship and witness more effective.

The Lord's Great Commission to carry the Good

News of God in Christ to the people of the world, whether in distant places or destitute neighborhoods, is carried on primarily by lay persons. Doctors, and teachers, and social workers, Peace Corps workers abroad, and Vista workers at home, all might be called the tip of the iceberg. Hosts of other people, who do not even think of themselves as "missionaries," so live in the course of their daily pursuits, that they bear witness to the saving power of God. Paul describes this ministry as "ambassadors for Christ, God making his appeal through us" (II Corinthians 5:20).

How do we enlist for this ministry?

We enlisted when we were baptized. The bishop or the priest officiating placed his hand on our heads and made the sign of the cross on our foreheads—"marked as Christ's own forever." We were received into the house-hold of God as full-fledged members. The Lord's Great Commission and his injunction, "After you receive the Holy Spirit you are to be my witnesses," is, therefore, addressed to each newly-baptized individual just as it has always been addressed to every committed Christian of whatever age or generation. However, the baptized person may be an infant and his sponsors may be making the necessary promises on his behalf. The day will come when that child has matured and speaks up for himself as a responsible Christian. That latter occasion is marked by a service called Confirmation.

Confirmation. The Prayer Book rubric describes Confirmation in these words:

> In the course of their Christian development, those baptized at an early age are expected, when they are

ready and have been duly prepared, to make a mature
public affirmation of their faith and commitment to the
responsibilities of their Baptism and to receive the laying
on of hands by the bishop (BCP, pg. 412).

It is quite clear that Confirmation is in no sense a
completion of what took place when those persons were
baptized. It is, however, a significant occasion on which
those, baptized in infancy, seek the renewal of the
covenant entered into on their behalf by their sponsors.
Their commitment to Christ and his service is publicly
proclaimed. Then, after praying that God renew his
covenant with them, we pray that they go "forth in the
power of that Spirit to perform the service you set
before them" (BCP, pg. 418). Thus, mature Christians
are aware of their place in the ranks of the Lord's faithful followers, and of the strengthening power of God's
indwelling Spirit to live up to their profession. Confirmation, then, is, in a sense, the commissioning of a
mature, responsible Christian.

In the early Church, there was no clear distinction
drawn between Baptism and Confirmation since both
were part of the complex initiatory ceremony presided
over by the bishop which also included the Holy Eucharist. That melling is still evident, for when the bishop
takes part in the baptism of an adult he lays his hand on
the candidate's head and pronounces him "sealed by the
Holy Spirit." Some liturgical scholars, including some
members of the House of Bishops, consider Confirmation under these circumstances to be a redoing of what
has already taken place. However, it becomes a separate
rite when the bishop, the representative of the whole
Church, lays hands on the head of one who has been

baptized *previously* by a priest. It is then the means by which the gift of the Holy Spirit, given in Baptism, is renewed and the candidate is confirmed and strengthened by God's grace to live the life God sets before him.

There are two other appropriate uses of the Confirmation Rite.

(1) *Reception.* Suppose a person who has grown up in another branch of Christendom wishes to become a member of the Episcopal Church. He/she has already been baptized with water in the Name of the Father and of the Son and of the Holy Spirit. That person is already a full-fledged Christian, but the Church should highlight his/her joining the Episcopal Church as the beginning of a new chapter in that individual's spiritual life. So it is appropriate and desirable that he/she be presented to the bishop as representing the whole Church, and that the new relationship be blessed with the laying on of hands and a recommissioning to Christian service.

(2) *Reaffirmation.* Sometimes an individual, who was baptized and confirmed years back, becomes lax about his Christian commitment and responsibilities, then awakens to his obligations. He wishes to begin again, to renew his baptismal covenant, and to start his Christian life afresh. Such a one desires and is entitled to make a public witness to his now-seriously confessed faith and to receive the strengthening gifts of the Spirit for renewal. It is no small thing to realize that one has drifted away from loyalty to Jesus Christ the Lord and to wish to return. That spiritual milestone may now be witnessed to impressively in the presence of the bishop.

Thus, the Church marks the occasion when a mature person is enlisting for service to Christ and his kingdom by a rite in which the strengthening gifts of the Spirit are bestowed by the bishop in the laying on of hands. For some, it is the occasion for confirming the promises made by sponsors on their behalf at their baptism, for others it may be the moment when they are received into this branch of the one holy catholic and apostolic Church, and for still others it is the occasion of their serious renewal and rededication. In each case the person is sent forth by God "in the power of that Spirit to perform the service he sets before them" (BCP, pg. 418). He has enlisted with those who seek to carry out the Great Commission.

Chapter 24

Our Ministry of Prayer

At the conclusion of the Baptismal Service in the first Prayer Book (1549), there was an exhortation to God-parents regarding the Christian upbringing of their Godchild which included "that they may learn the Creed, the Lord's Prayer, and the Ten Commandments, in the English tongue, and all other things which a Christian ought to know and believe to his soul's health." That exhortation appeared in every succeeding revision of the Prayer Book in one form or another through the 1928 revision. This requirement is implied in the present Prayer Book in the questions in The Baptismal Covenant when a person is baptized (BCP, pgs. 304-305). The change was made because literalists misconstrued their meaning and fell into thinking that one could become a Christian merely by learning appropriate phrases. Actually, Creed, Lord's Prayer, and Ten Commandments are symbols, symbols of what a Christian believes, how he prays, how he behaves. They are important as indicating the way in which a Christian should go.

We examined the Creed in Chapter 18. Let's now look at the Lord's Prayer, and, in the next chapter, the Ten Commandments.

The Lord's Prayer is the only prayer Jesus ever taught his followers. There are two versions of it in the Gospels (Matthew 6:9-13 and Luke 11:2-4). They differ somewhat because the prayer had undergone some editing and modification at the hands of scribes. Scholars generally agree that the original prayer was probably like this:

> Father, hallowed be thy Name.
> Thy kingdom come.
> Give us this day our daily bread
> and forgive us our debts, as we also forgive our debtors.
> And lead us not into temptation.

Any Jew could pray, "Our Father who art in heaven," using the formal, religious word *Abinu*. But Jesus uses *Abba* which is a child's address to his father. A better translation then would be "Daddy" or "Poppa." Jesus teaches his disciples to pray to God with simple family intimacy. And the prayer deals with the things a son or daughter needs to say to a parent. First there are the Father's larger concerns, then personal needs.

God's Name involves his whole nature and purpose. To pray, "Hallowed be thy Name," is to pray that it be venerated, known, and held in reverence. This is a petition that God act to display his holiness and love which, of course, requires human agents and a human response, so it is also a prayer of dedication.

The second great concern is for the coming of God's kingdom, his rule of righteousness and love that he will establish in his own good time. There is no contradiction between this prayer and the fact that as the Gospel makes clear the kingdom had arrived in the person of Jesus. The rule of God was perfectly present in him, but it must grow and spread until it embraces all people. Here again, our dedication and service are involved.

Now the prayer shifts from these larger concerns of

the Father of us all to our individual needs. The first is, "Give us this day our daily bread." We are asking the heavenly Father for sustenance in order that we may have the strength to cope during this day. As for the future, we trust it to his good providence. The more mature we become the more we pride ourselves on our self-sufficiency and our ability to provide for tomorrow and its emergencies. The Lord is teaching us to trust God for the morrow that we cannot guarantee. Our abilities and foresighted planning must never blind us to our fundamental need to rely on God's love and mercy, and to thank him for his care. John Henry Newman put it this way:

I do not ask to see the distant scene;
One step enough for me. (Hymn 430, The Hymnal 1940)

The petition challenges us to trust in God.

Our second individual need is for forgiveness. "Forgive us our debts as we also forgive our debtors." Forgiveness is not bestowed because we are forgiving as a condition to be met or a price to be paid. Rather, God's forgiveness is freely given, but can only be received by those who are open to it because they are forgiving. Such people understand what it costs to forgive and so appreciate it and treasure it. The Father of all wants us back in the family circle (which is what forgiveness means), but we have to want to be with the other members of the family otherwise we cannot accept his forgiveness. Suppose the Prodigal Son had had a fight with his elder brother and that was why he asked for his inheritance and left home. When he returned, his father would welcome him with open arms, but he would say to him, "I'll be delighted to have you back in the family, but can you get along with your Brother Jack?" That is what "Forgive us as we forgive" is all about.

The last personal concern is for protection—"Lead us not into temptation." All of us need protection from any situation that would overpower our strength of character. That kind of temptation is all around us. A young athlete knows that with a little cheating he is certain to pass the crucial examination and so be able to stay on the team. A young woman feels sure she could pass a required course by having her bright roommate write that term paper for her. The person who is having a very hard time making ends meet handles a great deal of cash in the course of his daily work. The world in which we live tempts us at every turn and so we pray, "Lead us not into temptations which may be too hard for us, but whatever comes deliver us from evil."

So we are praying that the heavenly Father be reverenced, that his will and purposes be known and carried out by all people, and that we have a share in bringing that about. Then, for ourselves, we pray for the capacity to put our trust in him, to be open to his forgiveness, and to live under his protection. Such is the prayer our Lord gave us.

The Lord's Prayer, as we said, is a symbol of how a Christian prays. The Prayer Book lists these principal kinds of prayer: adoration, praise, thanksgiving, penitence, oblation, petition, and intercession (BCP, pg. 856). Here are some examples:

Praise and adoration—*Benedictus es, Domine,* pg. 49; *Gloria in excelsis* and *Te Deum Laudamus,* pg. 52,

Penitence—pgs. 320-321 and 447-452,

Oblation—pg. 336,

Thankgiving—pgs. 836-841,

Petitions for ourselves and loved ones—pgs. 828-833, 458-461,

Intercessions for others—There is a good list of categories of people who need our prayers on page 383.

Of course no one ever prays for all these people and needs, nor is expected to, but these lists may whet our imagination. Pray only for those persons and needs that are real and genuine to you, and sum up all the rest by saying the Lord's Prayer slowly and thoughtfully.

One more word—form the habit of praying in the morning just as soon as you get up. Otherwise, in spite of your good intentions, your prayers will get crowded out of your day. There are lots of occasions for little sentence prayers during the day—while you wait for a traffic light, or bus, or elevator, for example—but don't let these take the place of your regular morning prayers. Then, at night, just before you get in bed hand the whole day back to God. Thank him for the good things and tell him you are sorry where you have messed it up. These are only suggestions. Your priest is the person with whom to discuss what would be the best discipline of daily prayer for you.*

But know this: *Life is full of wonders for the person who prays regularly.*

---

*Many of the insights in the discussion of the Lord's Prayer came from G. B. Caird, *The Gospel of St. Luke,* The Pelican New Testament Commentaries series (Middlesex, England: Penguin Books, 1971), pgs. 151-153.

Chapter 25

Our Ministry of Witness

Taking the Ten Commandments seriously is one way others know we mean what we say we believe. Let's seek to discover why the little document by that name has influenced human conduct for well over 3000 years.

First, the name: *Commandments.* These are not impersonal-like laws or rules. They are not good ideas which someone recommends. "Command" means that someone in authority directs and requires action by the person addressed. There are two listings of the Ten Commandments in the Bible—Exodus 20:1-17 and Deuteronomy 5:6-21—and there is no question but that God is speaking to his people. Instead of "Thou shalt" and "Thou shalt not" read "You shall" and "You shall not." The Lord God is speaking to You . . . to Me. This is a no-nonsense directive. He does not say, "I suggest" or "It would be a good idea if," rather he says, "You shall/shall not." There are no exceptions, no loopholes. So we take the Ten Commandments very seriously.

The question comes to mind: Why would we want to obey them quite apart from the fact that the Lord has told us to? The answer is gratitude. "I am the Lord your God, who brought you out of the land of Egypt, out of the house of bondage, (therefore)" and then follow the Commandments. They were the way the Israelites could

119

show their gratitude for having been delivered from Egyptian slavery. And, when Paul and other Christian missionaries wrote to struggling little churches, they also put ethics in the context of gratitude: because of what God in Christ has done for you, this is the way you should behave to show your gratitude. "Biblical ethics," said Theodore Wedel, "is therefore ethics" (Deuteronomy 4:37, 40; Romans 12:1; Ephesians 4:1).

Let's now take a closer look at the Commandments. The first four tell us what our duty is toward God; the last six tell us of our duty toward our neighbors. (The Prayer Book lists the Ten Commandments in traditional language on pages 317-318, and in contemporary English on page 350.) Succinctly, the catechism explains their meaning in this way (BCP, pgs. 847-848):

Our duty is to believe and trust in God;

    I To love and obey God and to bring others to know him;

    II To put nothing in the place of God;

    III To show God respect in thought, word, and deed;

    IV And to set aside regular times for worship, prayer, and the study of God's ways.

Our duty to our neighbors is to love them as ourselves, and to do to other people as we wish them to do to us;

    V To love, honor, and help our parents and family; to honor those in authority, and to meet their just demands;

    VI To show respect for the life God has given us; to work and pray for peace; to bear no malice, prejudice, or hatred in our hearts; and to be kind to all the creatures of God;

VII To use all bodily desires as God intended;

VIII To be honest and fair in our dealings; to seek justice, freedom, and the necessities of life for all people; and to use our talents and possessions as ones who must answer for them to God;

IX To speak the truth, and not mislead others by our silence;

X To resist temptations to envy, greed, and jealousy; to rejoice in other people's gifts and graces; and to do our duty for the love of God, who has called us into fellowship with him.

The Commandments have been summarized variously. One summary is these two sentences:

    I There is one God
   II   only
  III who must be revered and
  IV   worshiped regularly.
    To be his faithful servants we must
   V honor our parents and
  VI   not kill,
 VII   commit adultery,
VIII   steal,
  IX bear false witness, or
   X   covet.

John H. Westerhoff summarizes the Commandments in this thought-provoking way: In the first four we learn that we are not God. Since this is so, the last six show us the way to live, get along, and not destroy each other.

Jesus summarized the Commandments by quoting the two great commandments of the Old Testament: "Thou shalt love the Lord thy God with all thy heart, and with all thy soul, and with all thy mind. This is the first and great commandment. And the second is like unto it: Thou shalt love thy neighbor as thyself. On these two commandments hang all the Law and the Prophets.'' (Matthew 22:37-40; see also Deuteronomy 6:4 and Leviticus 19:18)

When you come down to it, we don't ever succeed in living up to God's Commandments whether as the Ten Commandments or as our Lord's summary. But this does not have to be a reason for discouragement. It only points up the fact that we are sinners and that all of us need the redeeming love of God which came to us in Jesus Christ who died for our sins and rose again to give us, through his Church, his own victorious Spirit.

When we take the Commandments seriously, we then hear great good news in the words, "For God so loved the world that he gave his only Son, that whoever believes in him should not perish but have eternal life" (John 3:16). This realization causes us to ask

How can I repay thy love,
Lord of all the hosts above?
What have I, a child, to bring
Unto thee, thou heavenly King?

I have but myself to give:
Let me to thy glory live;
Let me follow, day by day,
Where thou showest me the way.

(Hymn 239, The Hymnal 1940)

Christian behavior is the Christian's way of saying, "Thank you," to the Heavenly Father. "Father of all mercies . . . give us that due sense of all thy mercies . . . that we [may] show forth thy praise, not only with our lips, but in our lives'' (BCP, pg. 58-9).

The way you and I behave bears witness to the Good News of God which comes to us in Jesus Christ our Lord.

Chapter 26

Our Wider Ministry

When we decide to take seriously our Lord's Great Commission, we begin to realize how immense that commission really is. "Go and make disciples of *all nations,* baptizing them" in the Name of the Holy Trinity. How can an insignificant person like me possibly do anything like that? Most of us don't even know how to begin to make disciples of the people on our block or in our apartment building, to say nothing of those in our school or where we work. The job of being a practicing Christian is so unrealistically big that we are discouraged before we begin. How can we possibly take the Lord's directive seriously?

Martin Luther wrote a hymn which contained the words:

"Did we in our strength confide,
Our striving would be losing."
(Hymns 687, 688, The Hymnal 1982)

How right Luther was. Because Jesus was well aware of that fact, too, when he, the risen Lord, appeared to the disciples, he bestowed his Spirit on them. It was the same Spirit that the account of his baptism describes as having descended upon him like a dove from heaven. That Holy Spirit had been the motivating power of his life and ministry; now, it had been given to his apostles. Moreover, when others joined the company of believers, the newly-formed Christian Church, they were not only baptized in the Name of the Father and of the Son and of the Holy Spirit, but the apostles' hands were laid on them and they, too, received the Holy Spirit. That is what Christian baptism was from the beginning. That is what it is today. That is what it was when *you* were baptized. In Confirmation you acknowledge publicly that at baptism God gave you all the equipment you need to serve him faithfully, and you promise to do just that: be faithful.

Just as our bodies need food in order to grow and be strong, so also do our spiritual lives. In order for us to continue to serve God faithfully and well, the Church provides the sacrament of the Holy Eucharist for the continual "strengthening of our union with Christ and one another," and as a "foretaste of the heavenly banquet which is our nourishment in eternal life" (BCP, pg. 860). Faithful weekly attendance at the Lord's Supper is not just a part of a rule of life—an outwardly imposed obligation, it is the necessary pattern of spiritual behavior of a healthy church person who wants to have the strength to serve the Lord as best he/she can. Read what we say earlier about a person's preparation before coming to the Eucharist (Chapter 20). The benefits derived from the sacrament are likely to be greater if we are prepared in heart and mind to receive "the bread of life" and "the cup of salvation."

It is now, with open eyes, that we view the task Christ committed to his Church and to each of us as conscientious members of that Body of Christ. We know that the

Lord's Spirit will sustain our efforts to serve him. The time has come to be specific: What am *I* going to do as *my* Christian witness to try to be faithful to Jesus Christ my Lord and Savior?

If a pebble is dropped into a still pool of water, circles of ripples develop and become wider and wider. The exercise of our Christian ministry is similar to that. When we first begin to consider ways in which we may be Christ's faithful followers, we think about what we can do at home, in the neighborhood, at school, among our friends, on our job. Remember what was said about the ministry of lay persons in the last chapter. This is a start, but the time comes when we realize that our Christian responsibility does not stop with those whom we can touch and see. Wider circles of Christian witness are our responsibility also.

There are people in other neighborhoods, in other cities and villages, in far away places who have never heard the Good News of God's love or that he sent his Son in order that they might have life in all of its abundance and, beyond the grave, life everlasting. Those distant folk deserve to know of that Good News. We cannot reach them in person, but the Church can. The Church has work in prisons, on college campuses, among immigrant farm workers, in lonely Arctic villages, and in thatched-roof tropical settlements. It supports such projects as a medical clinic in Alaska, a college in Liberia, relief of earthquake victims in Central America, and famine relief in East Africa and southeast Asia, to name but a few. Giving to the work of the Church and its mission is a way to extend our Christian witness far beyond the reach of our hands and the sound of our voices.

When you think about it, the money you give to the Church represents a bit of yourself. For example, suppose you work for $5.00 an hour. At the end of a day all you have to show for eight hours of your productive existence is $40. Now suppose on Sunday you put $5.00 in the alms basin. That $5.00 represents one hour of your life. You have given one hour of yourself to the Lord and his Church for use in his service. That $5.00 can now be sent to the end of the earth and translated into Christian service. That is why giving to the work of the Church is important to each of us—a part of us is being invested in serving the Lord in some distant place.

The needs of those for whom we care we hold up before God in our prayers. We pray for the members of our family who have special need—sickness, affliction of some kind, an overwhelming problem—and ask the merciful, almighty Lord to strengthen and relieve them. Our concerned prayers bind us closer both to our merciful Lord to our needy loved ones. We stand with them and the merciful goodness of God touches us both. "The prayer of a righteous person has great power in its effects," wrote an early Christian leader (James 5:16) out of his experience, and it is just as true today.

Now, as Christians, we members of the Family of God are concerned for the welfare of his other children wherever they may be, however, distant. We pray that God's will be done on earth, that people everywhere may have an opportunity to experience that life in all of its fullness which our Lord came to make possible. This is the meaning of the Lord's Prayer petition, "Thy kingdom come." With the ultimate coming of the Heavenly

Father's rule of righteousness and love that glorious day will arrive. Praying for others is one of the ways in which every responsible member of the Church can serve the Father of us all regularly, faithfully, and well.

We who are confirmed, or are about to be, take seriously our Christian duty as it is spelled out in the Catechism:

> The duty of all Christians is to follow Christ; to come together week by week for corporate worship; and to work pray, and give for the spread of the kingdom of God (BCP, pg. 856).

In Confirmation we are aware that we have the strengthening gift of God's Holy Spirit, the needed power from on High, to perform our Christian duty.

APPENDIX: LEADER'S GUIDE

When we begin to think about Confirmation instruction for young people here is the picture into which we are intended to fit. The Confirmation rubric (BCP, pg. 412) states:

> In the course of their Christian development, those baptized at an early age are expected, when they are ready and have been duly prepared, to make a mature public affirmation of their faith and commitment to the responsibilities of their Baptism and to receive the laying on of hands by the bishop.

So the purpose of Confirmation instruction for young people is to help them begin to be responsible Christians in their own right, and to give them the information persons their age need to assume their rightful, responsible place in the life of the Church.

There are several key words and phrases here which we need to keep in mind. It is important that young people are "ready" and are prepared in heart and mind to kneel before the bishop to receive the laying on of hands. It is important also that the instruction has helped "them begin to be responsible Christians *in their own right.*" After all these years since the crucifixion-resurrection, the Christian faith is vital because it is the Good News of God's love and redeeming power to all kinds of people, including early adolescents, in every generation.

Don't fall into the satanic trap of thinking that "ready and duly prepared" means cramming young heads full of facts which may seem irrelevent to them. Surveys show that Confirmation instruction often gives a smattering of information on every aspect of Christian thought and practice—a capsule three-year seminary course—intended to be absorbed by young people in a matter of weeks. (One course uncovered by a diocesan survey listed some 23 different subjects!) Accent on persons can be Christian *Good* News; accent on facts can come across to youngsters as Christian *Bad* News.

Our goal is to try "to help them *begin* to be responsible Christians in their own right, and to give them the information *people of their age* need to assume their rightful, responsible place in the life of the Church." With this goal in mind the accent mark of our instruction will fall in a different place than it would if the class were composed of young adults or middle-aged persons. For example, in dealing with Baptism much more class time needs to be spent on discovering the relevance of the questions that are part of the Baptismal Covenant than in grappling with the mystery and wonder of Baptism as a sacrament. Your youngsters are struggling to be persons in their own right. The insights they gain from such a class on the Baptismal questions may help them become Christian persons in their own right. This course should provide your young people with what they need to know about the faith of their fathers that will give meaning and purpose to their lives *now.*

First century Christians were concerned that their children be faithful to the risen Lord. They could not merely prepare their children in the ways of future discipleship because derision, even persecution, were ever-present possibilities for young Christians as well as for old. Here is advice given early Christian parents on bringing up their children:

> Fathers, do not provoke [frustrate with too great demands] your children, lest they become discouraged (Colossians 3:21).
> Bring them up in the discipline and instruction of the Lord (Ephesians 6:4).

The Greek word translated "discipline" in the foregoing RSV quotation is given as "nurture" in the King James Version—or as the dictionary puts it, "that which nourishes." Its meaning is the same as that in an earlier chapter dealing with men's relations to their wives which are described in terms of the Lord's relation to the Church—he "nourishes and cherishes" it (Ephesians 5:28-29).

All this is saying that our responsibility toward our children is to help them to be faithful children of God and to teach them by providing them "that which nourishes" suitable to their needs and capacities. Beware lest we do the opposite! Pray do not succumb to the demonic temptation to frustrate them by feeding them "gagging" quantities of information about the Christian faith. As a result of such treatment they become discouraged—discouraged enough to turn their backs on the Church the instant they are free to go their own way.

Our purpose in Confirmation instruction, then, is, as we stated at the beginning, *to help them begin to be responsible Christians in their own right, and to give them the information people their age need to assume*

their rightful, responsible place in the life of the Church.
Here are some suggestions which may help you achieve your purpose.

OVERALL PLANNING

Generally speaking, each chapter of the book covers a subject. This may be enough material for one session or several, or for only part of one session. Classes move at different speeds because the details of one subject may be more important in one parish than in another. Only you and your class can determine how much ground you will cover in a session. Also, the order in which the class considers each subject is your decision. The order of this book is in the framework of a search—what one first sees, a search for its essential meaning, and finally commitment. The subtitle pages make this clear (pgs. 1, 57, and 107). Some other scheme may seem more logical to you and your class. You decide.

You will, perhaps, wish to take your class on a number of "field trips." I suggest one for your initial session—a look at the outside of the church building. Other such expeditions may also prove valuable—an exploration of the interior of the church, its furniture and symbols, a meeting with a member of the Altar Guild to see the various church hangings and vestments. When considering the ordained ministry invite the rector to come to the class and tell them what he does all week. These and other change-of-pace activities will help to enliven your class.

Put a lot of time, and thought, and prayer—a lot of yourself—into your overall planning and your preparation for each session. You will succeed, your children will find it interesting, and both of you will learn a great deal. There is profound truth in Paul's dictum, "Let him who is taught the word share all good things with him who teaches" (Galatians 6:6).

SOME TEACHING PROCEDURES

A few years back, a group of educators were planning a religious television program for children. Several children were invited to criticize the pilot program in which an adult was teaching a group of very quiet and well-behaved children. A nine-year-old boy put his sage criticism in a question, "Mr. Johnson, don't you know that children learn when children talk?"

The temptation is to tell the class a lot of valuable and essential information. A question that can be answered with a fact is not discussion. "Why" and "What do you think . . ." questions are more likely to get them involved in the subject at hand, but it is even better if the questions come from members of the class. Here are some ways to bring that about.

Listen Posts—Divide the class in four groups. During your presentation of the day's subject have each group listen for one thing:

1. Information we do not understand;
2. Something we would like to hear more about;
3. Ideas we agree with;
4. Things we think were left out.

After your presentation (limited carefully to 15 minutes) have each group meet for a few minutes and then report. Now you can go on for another 10 minutes with your further comments and explanations.

No matter how large the class, never have more than four groups. If possible, do not have less than four persons to a group. Maybe class size will permit you to have only three groups. If the class is fewer than eight, ask each person to listen attentively then write one question he would like you to answer on the subject.

For the individual questioners, you might post the listen post topics and let them address their question to one of them.

Panel Discussion—Divide the class into groups. Ask each group to select one person to be on a panel where he will ask the questions which are of concern to members of his group as well as his own. The panel is to be composed of the group representatives and yourself. Conduct a question-and-answer session and a discussion. The questions and the discussion do not need to stay on the subject of the day nor do they need to be limited just to members of the panel. Others may enter in if they have something to say. The groups, of course, are to be determined before your presentation begins.

Opinion Blanks—During the last few minutes of each session have each person fill out an opinion blank and turn it in *unsigned*. That blank reads as follows with plenty of space for answers:

1. Today's class was (good   )
                    (not so good) because:

2. Something I didn't have a chance to say (or want to ask out loud):

3. Something I didn't understand:
4. Something I heard you say:

Explain that this is not a test of the members of the class, rather it is a test of the teacher, so they do not have to sign their names. Ask them to take it seriously because you want to learn how to do a good job as teacher. Explain that they do not have to write something in every blank, but that everyone is expected to write something. At the beginning of the next session spend ten minutes dealing with the questions and topics on last week's opinion blanks.

SUGGESTED SESSION OUTLINES

First Session—

4:00 p.m. Opening prayer. Spend some time getting acquainted. Get each child's name and nickname, pleasantly and informally, so that everyone hears his own voice. Make any necessary preliminary announcements (Usually, announcements can be posted in large print and referred to only.)

4:10 p.m. Tell class members about the course and what will be expected of them—regular attendance, two book reports, memory work, and a final examination. Expect abysmal groans. Assure them that everyone can pass if he tries regardless of whether he does well in school or not. This course is serious business to you and you hope it will be to them, but it can be fun, also.

4:15 p.m. Give everyone a book. Explain that we are entering upon an exploration together. Read the Part I subtitle page. Present the material in chapters 1 and 2.

4:25 p.m. Take the class out into the church yard to discover what is alike and different from the presentation just made.

4:45 p.m. Return to the classroom. Ask if anyone has anything to share as a result of what was discovered outside. If they do, let them talk about it. If no one speaks up, introduce the Opinion Blank, explain carefully and have everyone fill out one and turn it in.

5:00 p.m. Adjourn.

Other sessions after the initial "get-acquainted" session—

4:00 p.m. Opening prayer; call attention to the posted announcements.

4:03 p.m. Discuss the previous session's Opinion Blank questions and comments.

4:18 p.m. Set up class participation procedure (Listening Posts or groups for later Panel Discussion). The first time explain carefully and be certain everyone understands. After the first time this should take only about two minutes.

4:20 p.m. Presentation of the day's topic.

4:35 p.m. Class discussion of the subject in their assigned groups.

4:45 p.m. Answer questions that arise in the small groups.

4:57 p.m. Opinion Blanks.

5:00 p.m. Adjourn.

HOMEWORK

The easy assumption is that it is a lost cause to expect
to have early teenagers do any homework because of
their school demands and the like. False. You told them
at the beginning that Confirmation is serious business.
Requiring and expecting them to take outside assign-
ments seriously will gain respect both for the course and
for you as the teacher. I recommend memory work and
outside reading.

Memory Work

For generations our Church has listed the Creed, the
Lord's Prayer, and the Ten Commandments as memory
work required before Confirmation. Other possible
memory work might include those parts of the regular
services of the Church that the congregation says in
unison. Such things as the General Confession, the
Gloria, the General Thanksgiving, the *Gloria in excelsis,*
and the *Nunc dimittis.* Consider including some important Bible verses, such as Matthew 28:18-20, John 3:16,
and Acts 1:8. The Catechism (BCP, pgs. 845-862) also
contains material you may want them to learn. Here are
those sections of the Catechism which are directly related
to the material in specific chapters:

Chapter 8—The Holy Eucharist
Chapter 16—The Church
Chapter 17—The Old Covenant
                The New Covenant
                Holy Scriptures

Chapter 18—The Creeds
          God the Father
          God the Son
          The Holy Spirit
Chapter 20—The Sacraments
          Holy Baptism
          The Holy Eucharist
          Other Sacramental Rites
Chapter 21—The Ministry
Chapter 24—Prayer and Worship
Chapter 25—The Ten Commandments

These are only suggested lists from which to choose. Some of the Catechism material might be used more profitably in class discussion.

One way to handle memory work is to give out the required list early in the course and, before the series of classes is over, have each participant turn in a statement signed by a godparent or an adult friend indicating that the young person has learned the material. Since the course is intended to be preparation for becoming a responsible member of the Church, I advise against having a parent hear his child's memory work. A parent will take over responsibility for seeing that the child learn the material. You are trying to train youngsters to be responsible, not parents.

Outside Reading

Assign two books and one of the Gospels to be read in the course of the series of classes—this book, the basis of the course, and a book telling the story of the Gospel of our Lord as well as one of the Gospels. Here is a procedure which has worked for others in getting this done.

So far as this book is concerned, ask the class to keep pace with the subjects discussed each session by reading the appropriate chapter or chapters in the text book. Tell them to read each chapter, to think about it, and then to write one test question which would cause the people taking the test to think. Caution them that they are not trying to catch those persons with some obscure detail, but trying to make them think. After the last session have class members turn in their list of examination questions on this book.

Confirmation instruction is of necessity mostly about the Church and its life and practices. Don't forget, however, we are trying to guide young people in becoming mature Christians who nurture their commitment to Jesus Christ in the life of the Church. These are among the opening words of the Confirmation Service:

Bishop: Do you renew your commitment to Jesus Christ?

Candidate: I do, and with God's grace I will follow him as my Savior and Lord.

Our course of instruction must not become so "churchy" that we overlook this fundamental. It is the dedicated follower of our Lord who is the good churchperson. That is why reading a book on the life of our Lord along with readings from the New Testament is essential. William Barclay, *The Life of Jesus for Everyman* (New York: Harper & Row, 1966) will give them an introduction to the Gospel story. After reading each chapter read the following New Testament passages:

after chapter 1—Luke 2:40-52
Mark 1:1-11

after chapter 2—Luke 4:1-13
      Mark 1:12-3:19

after chapter 3—John 1:1-14
      Mark 4:1-9, 26-41
        5:1-43
        6:1-30

after chapter 4—Mark 8:27-11:10, 15-19
        12:1-12
        14:1-72
        15:1-47

after chapter 5—Mark 16:1-8
      I Corinthians 15:3-8
      Luke 24:13-35

after chapter 6—Philippians 2:5-11
      II Corinthians 5:17-20
      Matthew 28:18-20

I suggest that youngsters use some modern translation such as the Good News Bible.

Here is a suggested procedure. About midway of the course give them this assignment and require their written report three or four weeks later. That report might follow this pattern. When you assign the book provide them with a series of test questions, one on the subject matter of each chapter in Barclay's book and/or the accompanying New Testament readings. After reading a chapter and the New Testament passages have them write out the answer to the question on that chapter. (Because of the arrangement of Barclay's book, more Marcan material is appropriately read following chapters 3 and 4. Therefore, you may want to give 2, or perhaps 3, questions after each of these chapters.) Give them questions which will make them think. Allow class members to work with the book open and the Bible in hand, and allow them to talk to whom they like. (They will learn a lot, and so will you.)

MAKE-UPS AND FAILURES

You told them at the beginning that you considered this course important business and that you expected them, also, to consider it that way. You will demonstrate this attitude by starting and stopping your class on time and by your solicitous concern for absentees. (A phone call the day the class met telling the absentee that you missed him is a good procedure.) If a person is late habitually or absent frequently, talk to *him* privately (*not* to his parents). After the series is over have required make-up sessions for absentees. If a youngster has not done the work and does not deserve to be confirmed along with the others, sit down with that individual. This is a pastoral matter. Why wasn't he interested? Your fault? his? parents? Would it be fair to the others to present him for Confirmation? What does he think you should do about his situation? Care about him. Remember the loving kindness of the Lord who said, "As the Father sent me even so send I you." Don't make the decision that he not be confirmed an authoritative pronouncement. Ask him if he wants any help in explaining the situation to his family. The parental tears when the bishop comes may be those of hurt pride, but experience has shown that that youngster will be the proudest member of the *next* class presented to the bishop.

FINAL EXAMINATION

The value of a final examination is that it can help you learn what each child is thinking. You will know already from class discussion and the opinion blanks (even though unsigned) whether they have absorbed information. I suggest an examination like this. Let them take it home and mail in their paper by a certain date.

1. Why do Episcopalians have a Confirmation Service?
2. What do you consider the most important thing you heard or read in this course?
3. Has some (any?) of what you have learned about the Episcopal Church agreed with what you have experienced and observed?
4. How would you persuade someone your age to come to Confirmation classes?

The examination papers are likely to be a pleasure to read, and full of surprises.